The Manager's Guide to Building a Successful Business

The Manager's Guide to Building a Successful Business

Gary Randazzo

business**expert**
Press

The Manager's Guide to Building a Successful Business

First published in 2013 by
Business Expert Press, LLC
222 East 46th Street, New York, NY 10017
www.businessexpertpress.com

ISBN-13: 978-1-60649-650-3 (paperback)

ISBN-13: 978-1-60649-651-0 (e-book)

Business Expert Press Entrepreneurship and Small Business Management collection

Collection ISSN: 1946-5653 (print)
Collection ISSN: 1946-5661 (electronic)

Cover design and interior design by Exeter Premedia Services Private Ltd., Chennai, India

First edition: 2013

10 9 8 7 6 5 4 3 2 1

Printed in the United States of America.

For my wife, Sue, who has comforted my soul, given me a family, and always been at my side.

For William E. Martin for giving me opportunities early in my career and for being a mentor whose standards I have always tried to achieve.

Abstract

The Manager's Guide to Building a Successful Business uses real market examples to demonstrate the effective use of management and marketing principles. The book also introduces programs developed over a 40-year career to help manage all aspects of a business and to develop and execute marketing strategies.

Managers and executives will use this book as a guide to grow an established business or start a new one. The book can be used as a reference book for unique management challenges as well.

The book differs from other business books in that it introduces management techniques and processes and shows how they are critical to executing successful marketing strategies. Each chapter covers a founding principle of management in Part I and a founding principle of marketing in Part II.

The examples used in the *Manager's Guide* are from large and small organizations in which the author was personally involved. The techniques introduced in the *Guide* are based on those studied at most universities. These techniques are used in solutions applied to challenges facing these organizations.

This book uses techniques described in Clayton Christensen's books on disruptive innovation as well as theories and techniques introduced by Frederic Herzberg, Abraham Maslow, Roger Wimmer, and Gerald Zaltman.

Key Words

planning, job performance, standards of performance, disruptive innovation, market disruptions, cash flow, PERT, pricing, marketing promotions, organizing, financial controls, motivating employees

Contents

Introduction

This book is an effort to connect the principles of marketing and management to the day-to-day business world use of those concepts.

What I have learned is that there is an ability to apply management and marketing principles in a methodical fashion to the business world and achieve real success.

This book is divided into the management sections that deal with planning, workforce, money, methods, directing and controls, and marketing sections that deal with price, place, product, and promotion. In each section, I use some of the projects I have worked on to demonstrate the principles and how they can be applied in the real world.

PART I

Management

This book starts with the principles of management and assumes that a business or an idea for a business exists. For an existing business, this section of the book provides direction for improving operations and expanding a business. For new business ideas and ventures, this section of the book provides the steps to build an infrastructure to successfully support a new enterprise.

CHAPTER 1

Planning

Vision and Mission Statement

Planning usually starts with a vision and mission statement. The clearer the vision and mission, the easier it will be to develop a plan to create an organization that will make the vision a reality.

If the vision and mission statement is too vague, it will be difficult to create a plan that will result in a clear direction for the enterprise. Similarly, too much detail in a vision and mission statement can limit the success of the enterprise.

In Houston, I work with a group of academicians and clinicians who are focused on creating a Research Institute to develop devices to deliver heath care to underserved populations affordably.

The following is a proposed mission and vision statement:

Telehealth Research Institute Mission and Vision Statement

Mission:

- To make available quality, affordable healthcare to all individuals worldwide
- To provide barrier breaking solutions to obstacles impeding the delivery of healthcare through the use of technology and telecommunications
- To create value and make a difference.

Vision: To create a collaborative network of clinicians, researchers, academicians and partners focused on creating modes of delivering affordable healthcare worldwide. This will be accomplished by:

- Attracting the best and brightest people to work in an environment that is challenging and rewarding

- Creating a network of technology and industrial partners that are focused on innovative solutions to healthcare delivery
- Establishing a center in Houston that serves as the worldwide center and incubator for telehealthcare solutions
- Working with hospitals and medical institutions worldwide to deploy new medical delivery innovations by technology and through telecommunications
- Working with industrial and financial partners to create new markets for telehealthcare delivery solutions
- Developing an organization that is highly effective, lean and fast moving.
- Maximizing long-term financial return for partners and long-term sustainability for the Telehealth Research Institute.

This mission and vision statement provides a framework that can be used to build a plan for the organization. On the basis of the aforementioned statement, it is apparent that the Research Institute will provide a place where physicians, engineers, academicians, and participants from industry can work together to develop products that can be commercialized. From here a planning group can begin designing the organization and start estimating resources that will be needed. They will also be able to identify activities that are required to put the organization into place.

At this stage of the process, it becomes very important to arrange activities in a fashion that allows for the most efficient use of resources and results in the envisioned enterprise within the timeframe and resources allotted. These activities will then become the basis of a planning process similar to the one that was used when we started the *Huntsville Morning News*.

P.E.R.T. PLANNING and *The Huntsville Morning News*

The use of the PERT (Project Evaluation and Review Technique that was developed by the U.S. Navy) approach in planning can provide a competitive advantage by keeping a project on schedule and within budgeted resource allocations.

I was approached by a group of businessmen to start a local newspaper in Huntsville, Texas, to compete with a corporate-owned newspaper.

Huntsville is a small college town north of Houston, Texas, and is the headquarters for the Texas Department of Corrections. Thus the economy, while small, is stable. The *Huntsville Item* was the local newspaper that was owned by the Harte Hanks Corporation. The *Item* was an afternoon newspaper and the dominant media outlet.

To be successful in launching a new newspaper, it would be critical to have a plan that would change the playing field and happen quickly enough that the *Item* would have a hard time responding.

After considering a number of options, we decided that we would start a morning newspaper that would be delivered to subscribers 7 days every week and that we would deliver our first newspaper 90 days after making the announcement. We would call our publication the *Huntsville Morning News*.

That is a pretty tall order even if you have a facility and equipment. It was an even bigger challenge for the *Morning News* considering we didn't have a building, land, presses, production equipment, or staff.

To develop a schedule and keep track of all the pieces of the plan, we used the PERT process. This approach requires managers to identify all tasks that need to be accomplished to complete a project. After the tasks are identified, they are arranged in a sequential order. The process also requires managers to identify which activities are dependent on other activities being completed (See Figure 1-1 for a task list).

For the *Morning News* we had to locate and buy land, get utilities to the land; construct a building; buy and install presses; buy and install editorial and prepress equipment; and hire editorial, accounting, circulation, advertising, and production staffs.

Since we had just 90 days, it was important to know how the project parts fit together. For example, we had to construct a building and, at the same time, install printing presses. We worked with the building contractor to put a roof over the press area before completing other parts of the building so the presses could have the maximum amount of time for installation.

Hiring and training the staffs were not dependent on the building but they did require some equipment. The approach here was to identify and order equipment while hiring staff so they would both be available at about the same time.

I am still amazed at the scope of the *Morning News* project and how well it came together. In 90 days after making the announcement, we delivered our first edition that was written and produced by our staff in our building on our presses. The PERT system was key to this accomplishment. An example of activities for a computer project using the PERT system is shown as follows.

Task	Earliest start	Length	Type	Dependent on...
A. High-level analysis	Week 0	1 week	Sequential	
B. Selection of hardware platform	Week 1	1 day	Sequential	A
C. Installation and commissioning of hardware	Week 1.2	2 weeks	Parallel	B
D. Detailed analysis of core modules	Week 1	2 weeks	Sequential	A
E. Detailed analysis of supporting modules	Week 3	2 weeks	Sequential	D
F. Programming of core modules	Week 3	2 weeks	Sequential	D
G. Programming of supporting modules	Week 5	3 weeks	Sequential	E
H. Quality assurance of core modules	Week 5	1 week	Sequential	F
I. Quality assurance of supporting modules	Week 8	1 week	Sequential	G
J. Core module training	Week 6	1 day	Parallel	C, H
K. Development and QA of accounting reporting	Week 5	1 week	Parallel	E
L. Development and QA of management reporting	Week 5	1 week	Parallel	E
M. Development of Management Information System	Week 6	1 week	Sequential	L
N. Detailed training	Week 9	1 week	Sequential	I, J, K, M

Figure 1-1. Task List: Planning a Custom-Written Computer Project. From Mind Tools—Reproduced with permission. http://www .mindtools.com/critpath.html

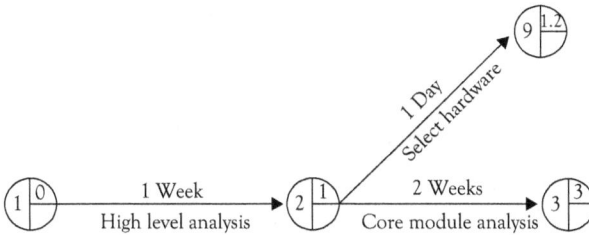

Figure 1-2. Circle and arrow Diagram showing two activities that cannot be started until the first activity has been completed. From Mind Tools—Reproduced with permission. http://www.mindtools .com/critpath.html

Plot the activities as a circle and arrow diagram (Figure 1-2).

Critical Path and PERT Analyses are presented using circle and arrow diagrams.

In these, circles show events within the project, such as the start and finish of tasks. The number shown in the left hand half of the circle allows you to identify each one easily. Circles are sometimes known as nodes.

An arrow running between two event circles shows the activity needed to complete that task. A description of the task is written underneath the arrow. The length of the task is shown above it. By convention, all arrows run left to right. Arrows are also sometimes called arcs.

This shows the start event (circle 1), and the completion of the create schedule (circle 2). Where one activity cannot start until another has been completed, we start the arrow for the dependent activity at the completion event circle of the previous activity.

Planning the Operations

With the activities and perhaps a PERT chart in hand, managers are now ready to make decisions on the inner workings of the organization by identifying how manpower, money, methods, and machinery will be best utilized to make the organization efficient and effective.

Decisions will have to be made to identify:

1. The type of workforce that will be needed and how the workforce will be managed. This will include the use of employees, contractors, and vendors.

2. The cash flows that will be needed to sustain the organization's operation. This will entail developing pricing strategies, sales quotas, credit,
accounts receivable programs, and accounts payable programs.

3. The type of policies and procedures that will govern how normal processes are employed and how out-of-the-ordinary situations are dealt
with. This will include inventory procedures and use of vendor programs such as just-in-time inventory and support promotion programs.

4. The type of equipment and space that will be needed and whether it
should be leased or purchased.

Planning Versus Budgeting

It is important to understand the difference between planning and budgeting. Planning is putting together actions and resources in order to accomplish an objective. A budget is a quantitative representation of the plan.
That is, you have to have a plan before you can budget. The better the plan is
thought out, the better the budget will be. The better the budget, the more
likely the outcome of the project will resemble that which was planned.

If yours is an existing operation and the plan is for one to five years, a
lot of the groundwork has been done. If yours is a new organization, all
of the preceding steps must be taken.

Many existing organizations create a budget that is based on the
preceding year's budget. This assumes, with the exception of new programs that are introduced, that the organization's goals are pretty much
unchanged. In many cases the new budget is just an iteration of the old
budget with the addition of some programs and personnel that are based
on expected growth. The expected growth is usually based on a projection
of past performance.

To be sure, this may be an acceptable approach for an organization
at the beginning of its or its industry's life cycle. But as an industry or a
corporation reaches a point where new innovation may change the landscape, this is a budgeting approach that can lead to trouble.

When budgeting is based on past performance, it promotes thinking and behavior associated with past performance. If an industry or
customer base expectations change, the organization will have a more
difficult time adjusting.

This is why organizations that do best in a changing environment do a better job of reviewing the marketplace frequently, assessing their approach, and revising their plan based on market changes. The planning process mirrors more closely the planning process of a new company.

The plan changes but not the company's overall vision and mission statement. The organization's mission statement may be the most important document for executive managers. It is critical that the mission statement be broad enough to allow for market changes but narrow enough to describe a business purpose.

For example, a mission statement that says the organization will produce a specific set of products and improve shareholder value by increasing profitability recognizes neither the business purpose nor the ability of the market to change.

A mission statement that says the organization exists to serve a specific market and its set of needs by providing high-value products and services recognizes the business purpose and indicates the organization and its products will change with the market needs.

If a well-designed mission statement guides the organization, the planning process will reflect the organization's focus on the market. Subsequently, the annual planning process will review how well aligned the organization is with market needs. The resulting business plan may show a decrease in resources allocated to products and projects with decreasing interest from the marketplace. The same plan is likely to show an increase in allocation of resources to new market opportunities.

The budgeting process that follows the annual plan allows a means of testing whether or not the plan is financially viable. For most companies, the budgeting process entails several draft budgets that are adjusted to insure the execution of the plan and provides a reasonable expectation that the financial results will be favorable.

Contingency Planning

Contingency planning is a backup plan that can be implemented if certain assumptions that guide the overall planning process change. For example, if revenues and staffing levels are based on a healthy economy in the overall plan, it may be wise to have a contingency plan should the economy soften.

The reason a contingency planning process should be considered is to make sure that thought has been given to prioritizing resource allocations when underlying assumptions change. The goal is to maintain financial integrity without changing the focus of the mission of the organization.

For example, if an organization has the mission to provide high-quality products and introduce new products continually, cash flows should be available for quality control and research and development. If sales suddenly drop due to an economic downturn, it would be important to find ways of increasing sales or reducing expense that did not involve price reductions or reductions in quality controls or research and development. Contingency planning allows managers to go through these potential scenarios in advance and have a plan and budget for success even when the environment changes.

CHAPTER 2

Workforce

Workforce planning for an organization can begin with the PERT chart developed in the initial stages of the planning process described in Chapter 1. These activities demonstrate the work that has to be done to get the organization operational. Once operational, there will be a minimum level of activity to keep the organization viable. This activity will determine the resources required.

Type of Workforce

When planning for an organization's workforce, it is useful to recognize the various sources of a workforce. All of the work does not have to be done by employees. Contractors, temporary help, service firms, and vendors can perform work.

Many companies have found that outsourcing call centers, accounting, and support functions improves service levels and reduces costs. Retailers provide shelf space for vendors' products in exchange for vendors stocking the stores' shelves.

Whether the work is accomplished by outside sources or employees, it will be important to find ways to ensure that those doing the work know what defines success and what role they play in moving the company forward.

What Employees Want

Research has shown that employers that successfully utilize hygiene and motivation factors in the workplace can have higher levels of productivity, lower levels of turnover, and employees with higher levels of self-esteem at work and home. These hygiene and motivation factors include the need to provide for basic survival and then security or job safety, a sense of belonging or acceptance, recognition, status, and self-actualization.

Assuming the basic survival needs have been addressed by compensation (the employee accepted the job at the offered pay rate), safety and security needs are the next to be addressed. Usually safety needs relate to job security, and an individual is more likely to feel secure if he or she feels he or she is performing as expected. Here the responsibility rests on the shoulders of the manager to clearly articulate how success on the job is achieved. An employee who has a clear understanding of what is expected will likely perform up to those expectations, which will, in turn, provide the manager with the results wanted and will result in the employee feeling secure in the knowledge that the performance requirements are being met.

Standards of Performance

The development of a program designed to address employee safety needs and meet organizational objectives can provide a productive workforce that makes significant organizational contributions.

The Corpus Christi Caller-Times *Standards of Performance*

The *Corpus Christi Caller-Times* newspaper was having difficulty with its financial reporting, and its payroll costs for the financial area seemed high.

After spending a few weeks with the personnel in the departments and reviewing operations, we felt that there was poor coordination between the various accounting functions and that there was duplication of effort. I was pondering an approach to address these challenges when I ran across an American Management Association workbook on "Standards of Performance." It suggested that a job should be broken down into responsibilities that related directly to organizational goals. Furthermore, it said that these responsibilities should have standards set that related directly to an employee's job performance.[1] The article also suggested job appraisals should be objective and directly related to the standards set.

It seemed that "Standards of Performance" would be a good way to provide the company with a clear path to achieving its goals while at the same time providing the employees with the ability to be secure in their position if they met their standards of performance.

Clearly, implementing the "Standards of Performance" program would be difficult. First, the employees were suspicious of any new program that focused on job performance. Second, to implement the program meant that we would have to sit down with each employee and understand how each task they performed related to the department's success and then set a mutually agreed upon standard for each task (See Exhibit I-2-1).

Exhibit I-2-1. Example of a Performance Standard.

Responsibility	Standard	Metric
1. Satisfied customers	No more than 10 customer complaints per quarter	0–2 = good 2–5 = acceptable 5+ = poor
2. Grow customer base	Net gain of 5 active accounts per quarter	5+ = good 2–5 = acceptable 0–1 = poor

The employees were more at ease when they were told the standards would be the basis for performance reviews and that standards would be mutually agreed upon. During meetings with each of the employees, we found that these individuals had a good feel of work that was being performed and of how the departmental objectives could be met. The result of the exercise was a group of employees who clearly understood their jobs and how to be successful in the job by meeting the standards set for each task.

The implementation of the "Standards of Performance" program resulted in a significant improvement in financial reporting and management of the company's financial assets. We also identified and eliminated information gathering and reporting that was either duplicated or not needed at all. In addition, as folks left or retired, we found that we were doing about twice the work more effectively with half the staff. We also found that the employees had a real sense of security and well-being because they understood the specific requirements to be successful in their jobs and received recognition as they achieved success.

This program also allowed us to understand the value of each job function and to establish benchmarks for pay rates that were meaningful to the employees and to the company.

From that point forward, I used the "Standards of Performance" program every opportunity I could. I felt like it worked for the employees and the company.

I think the greatest standards of performance success occurred at *the Houston Chronicle*. It was also the most difficult implementation. In my areas of responsibility, there were about 1,000 employees and about 2,500 independent contractors.

The Houston Chronicle *"Standards of Performance" Program*

The *Houston Chronicle* was very successful and had (during the same week I was named VP) just purchased the assets of the *Houston Post*, leaving the *Chronicle* the only major newspaper in the nation's fourth-largest city. The managers rightly felt like they had performed well enough to win a difficult market battle. As a result these seasoned managers felt like a "Standards of Performance" program would not bring benefits worth the efforts of implementation.

I felt that we had a lot of tough competition and that to garner a greater market share we would have to introduce new products and be very focused on organizational and financial goals. I really felt a "Standards of Performance" program would help with the focus.

The managers did not share my optimism. Indeed, the inertia was so great that I had to tell the division heads that I would not approve any performance reviews or salary adjustments if they were not accompanied by "Standards of Performance" worksheet for the position being reviewed. I said that this rule would go into effect in 6 months. Within 6 months, the *Houston Chronicle* had a "Standards of Performance" program for every position in the advertising, circulation, and marketing divisions.

To their credit, once the program was implemented, the managers took it to the next level by including training classes that would have to be completed for the individuals to hold their position and progress to new, more challenging positions. Bonus programs were tied directly to the same objectives as the standards of performance.

From the time of implementation to my departure 7 years later, revenues increased by 60%, and company profits more than doubled. That does not happen without folks who understand what must be done and are focused on successful execution.

Measurable Standards

One of the key elements of a sound "Standards of Performance" program is being able to measure the standards assigned. All jobs can be broken into elements that can be measured.

Exhibit I–2–2 below shows an example of a performance standard for a sales executive.

Before establishing metrics, it is important to understand how the job for which standards are being established fits into reaching the overall objectives of the organization. Just breaking a sales job down into accounts to be sold or number of customers served may be all that is needed if the organization is in a position that does not require new markets or new products.

To really understand if the job as it is currently defined fits into organizational goals, it is necessary to review the organization's goals and mission. If the organization's goals are to be the market leader and grow market share and profit levels of sales, the sales job will be different from an organization that wants to increase sales by 10% per year.

If an organization chooses a 10% revenue increase, establishing a 10% increase in sales volume with no rate increase will work.

But if growing market share and profitability are goals, the sales job tasks will be different. Here an element that requires growing new customers or introducing new products will be required. These sales job requirements will have implications for the marketing and new product development groups.

A job under the second scenario might require the sale of new products to new customers within the first 30 days of the new product's introduction to the market.

If a significant number of sales people missed this goal, it would signal the need for a product review.

Note that active accounts in Exhibit I-2-1 are different from new accounts in Exhibit I-2-2. To increase active accounts may mean convincing an account that has stopped buying to renew its relationship. To increase new accounts means to attract customers who have never bought from your organization.

Exhibit I-2-2. Example of a Performance Standard for a Growth Company.

Responsibility	Standard	Metric
1. Satisfied customers	No more than 10 customer complaints per quarter	0–2 = good 2–5 = acceptable 5+ = poor
2. Grow new customer base	Net gain of 5 new accounts per quarter	5+ = good 2–5 = acceptable 0–1 = poor
3. Develop new revenues from new customers from new products	Net gain of 5% per quarter	5+ = good 2–5 = acceptable 0–1 = poor

Results Without the "Standards of Performance" Program

One of the few times I did not use the "Standards of Performance" program was as general manager of the *San Francisco Chronicle*. I still believed in the need for all employees to be focused on organizational goals. This was an unusual situation in that Hearst had just purchased the *Chronicle* and sold their newspaper in the market, *The Examiner*. Both newspapers had been part of a Joint Operating Agreement (JOA) for the 35 years preceding the purchase of the *Chronicle* by Hearst. During the years under the JOA, not much attention had been given to the marketplace. In addition, the *Chronicle* was a union shop and each job had requirements based on union agreements. In my previous assignments, I had first reviewed the tasks being performed and made certain they tied to the organizational goals. Here I would not be able to create new standards tied to tasks but rather would have to create an organizational focus so compelling it would cause tasks to align with the organization's goals.

The challenge here was to get the organization to rise above the hurdles presented by the marketplace and friction with the unions. It appeared to me that we could only make real progress when employees and their unions recognized that a common focus was the only way to achieve success. I decided this focus had to be creating value for the customers of the newspaper, its readers, and advertisers. From the day I arrived until I left, every meeting I held and directive issued was aimed at getting management and labor to focus on the customer. As a result, employees from across the divisions began making suggestions to improve operations.

During this time, a number of successful new products were launched and unions made a number of changes that allowed the organization to be more responsive to the market. These new products and union changes were the result of people working toward a common goal—giving the customer real value. While a formal "Standards of Performance" was not employed, its principles were, and the results were positive.

Choosing Team Members

Aside from the "Standards of Performance" approach to providing security for employees and focus for the organization, it is important to build a team that is successful.

It is certain that we can break jobs down so they are easily understood and set standards for each task that tie directly to the organization's overall success. It is also certain that we can fill slots with individuals capable of understanding the job and operating at some acceptable level of performance.

An additional boost to organizational success is gained when individuals are chosen for positions based on how well their talents and interests match the tasks at hand.

For organizations that are performing below expectations, it might be a worthwhile effort to review employees' strengths and interests to see if they match well with the tasks they are assigned. There may be opportunities to improve performance simply by reassigning tasks and positions among current employees. Reassignment is usually preferable to replacing employees due to increased training costs and learning curves associated with new hires.

For organizations that are growing and need to add to staff, it is important to take great care in the hiring process. If the right individual is brought on board and trained properly, there is a good chance that even in business cycle downturns, the organization can perform well.

On the other hand, when business is very good and slots are filled without care, the organization is not likely to have the right people on board during downturns. This usually leads to layoffs, which has a negative impact on morale and overall performance.

Sales Force Requirements

While "Standards of Performance" and employee involvement are important in all aspects of the business organization, additional thought has to be given to the group that is its lifeblood—the sales force.

The most critical factor in having a successful sales force is choosing individuals who will be successful in a sales environment. These individuals should feel comfortable in approaching and talking to strangers. They should be able to engage in conversations and be good at listening. Individuals who will be successful in sales are also good at problem solving. A good sales person is able to meet a potential client, get that potential client to talk about their needs and find solutions to satisfy those needs.

If people filling sales positions do not have those characteristics, sales success will be limited to product strengths and market demand. This is an important distinction. Sales managers can at times have such great success with product benefits and market demand that they fill sales slots with people that interface well with customers and can fill orders accurately. These are known as order takers and fill an important role in organizations, but they are not sales people.

Sales people are much like entrepreneurs. They like to solve problems. They like to understand the full scope of their business and how it fits into the marketplace. They like to compete, and they like to win.

Directing a Sales Force

Successful direction of a sales force requires clearly establishing the parameters of success and ensuring the sales staff is properly trained. The most difficult part of a sales manager's job is identifying the tasks that will lead to success and measuring the level at which each sales person is performing those tasks. Identifying sales responsibilities is critical.

Those responsibilities include:

1. Product knowledge—can be determined through questionnaires administered after an indoctrination course.
2. Industry knowledge—can be determined through questionnaires administered after an indoctrination course.
3. Sales volume—For any business to be successful, a minimum sales volume must be attained and can be broken down to minimum sales volume per sales person per sales period.
4. Sales calls—To reach needed sales volumes, sales calls have to be made. Most organizations have statistics on number of calls made per successful sale that can be used as a target for the sales staff.
5. Account development—To grow, new customers added must exceed current customers that become inactive.
6. Customer satisfaction—This can be measured through customer surveys and customer complaints.

This list can be longer and more complex, but it must be clear and objectively measured. The sales manager and sales person must be able to look at the metrics and arrive at the same conclusions regarding goal attainment. The list of responsibilities should lend themselves to easily being incorporated into a "Standards of Performance" program.

Motivating a Sales Force

Successfully motivating a sales force requires the recognition that sales people will perform best when they are paid adequately, feel secure in their position, feel like they are part of the organization, receive recognition, and can grow professionally through the sales process.

Basic compensation is important and assures that individuals will be able to meet their basic financial (and physiological) needs. This can be accomplished by providing a base salary or a list of regular customers on which a commission is paid. Commission programs can provide basic income and incent sales people to find new customers as well. Components of the incentive program can focus sales people to increase the number of active customers per period or the revenue per customer per period. The basic salary and commission or both should provide a living wage with the ability to provide an income equal to that of successful sales people in other industries in the same market.

Security needs can be met through providing a reasonable amount of time for a sales person to achieve assigned sales goals. Sales people like a challenge but, as with all jobs, a new sales person will require an amount of time to become productive. Most companies have statistics on the length of time required to acquire sufficient product, company, and customer knowledge to be successful. Security needs can also be met through certain benefit programs such as health insurance and 401(k) programs.

Belonging needs can be met through sales meetings and company-wide meetings that create a camaraderie that is supported throughout the company. Good sales managers will recognize the importance of a sense of belonging and will work hard to ensure favoritism and unfair management practices do not impair team building.

Esteem and recognition can be accomplished through setting meaningful goals that are achievable. This can be a part of the commission program that focuses on new accounts, active customers per period, revenue per period per customer, multiple products per customer per period, and so on. Additional recognition programs for certain achievements can be held monthly, quarterly, or annually to further build esteem and recognition.

Using job promotions as a form of recognition should be used carefully. A good sales person does not necessarily make a good sales manager. It may be desirable to create several levels of sales positions if promotion is to be used as a form of recognition.

Self-actualization and growth can be accomplished by allowing sales people to help establish sales goals and "stretch goals," develop new sales approaches, and participate in new product design and pricing.

As a manager, it is important to approach staff motivation with a process that keeps a focus on the company and the sales staff. Programs should be designed within the company's financial wherewithal and in a staged approach. In other words, identifying responsibilities and standards should be implemented before motivational programs. Salaries and benefits should be within the company's financial capabilities and should be the first motivational/hygiene factors addressed.

If a company already has a stable sales force but needs to improve productivity, focus might be directed more to upgrading the "Standards of Performance" and recognition factors.

Additional motivational/hygiene factors can be implemented at any time but should not disrupt progress being made by the basic programs. These additional programs should be added when there is a tangible benefit that accrues to the organization and there is minimal disruption due to the implementation.

Creating a successful sales force is critical to the success of most companies. Screening and choosing qualified individuals and subsequent training is paramount.

Beyond screening and training, creating a successful sales team requires management to spend the time to clearly understand what is needed for the company to be successful and translate that to individual performance requirements. In addition, management must pay attention to the motivation and hygiene factors that will make sales people want to come to work in the morning and leave at the end of the day feeling good about their accomplishments and their company.

Each company will have a different set of challenges, and the approach to improving sales productivity will be different.

If a company chooses the right people, trains them, and manages through a focus on performance standards and hygiene factors, the chances for success are improved dramatically. In addition, the chances are increased that productivity will continue to be high over the long term and that employee morale will be high and turnover will be low.

Cross-Functional Teams

Theories on disruptive innovation hold that industry leaders grow their business based on the needs of their most profitable customers and revenue streams. Disruptive innovation occurs when a new technology appears on the scene that serves the industry's least profitable customer.

The industry leader finds that competing with a company targeting its least profitable customers is difficult due to the need for continued focus on the most profitable customers.

This is just one dilemma that is the result of value networks formed by industry leaders over time from a "hard wired" approach to problem solving within the industry that is based on experiences that have proven successful in the past.[2]

The inability to break away from approaches that have been "hard wired" into the organization can make it very difficult to effectively develop strategies to address disruptive technologies or to develop new product streams.

Most companies require new revenue and profit streams for growth and long-term success. If it is not developing new technologies, it is finding new markets for current technologies. Either approach requires new strategies and is based on innovative thinking. For new ideas to be incorporated into the "muscle" of the organization usually requires participation by all of the organization's functional groups—Finance, Marketing, Sales, Production, and Human Resources. This incorporation becomes difficult if it is at odds with the "hard wired" thinking.

Cross-Functional Teams at Corpus Christi Caller-Times

Cross-functional teams can provide options to "hard wired" approaches to problem solving and promote buy-in across the organization.

Beginning with my first assignment to review the market position of the *Corpus Christi Caller-Times* and to make recommendations on actions needed, I looked to a cross-functional task group for solutions. An assignment that might change things across an organization was daunting, and it was clear to me that I did not have enough knowledge of the organization's functions to determine the impact of any potential changes. A task group comprising individuals from across the organization would help combat inertia from "hard wired" approaches and would allow any new approaches to recognize organizational constraints, address weaknesses, and exploit organizational strengths.

Information presented to the task group showed the market comprised a growing number of small businesses that did not need and could not afford to have their advertising in the newspaper, which was distributed to subscribers across south Texas.

The financial data showed the economics of running the newspaper presses. Because the presses were large and required a significant work group to run, products produced needed to be printed in substantial quantities. This meant a high variable or direct cost and would require significant revenue streams. These revenue streams would not be possible to generate from the growing number of businesses that wanted to focus on the immediate markets around their business location.

Presented with this information and with some study of what was being done in other markets, the task group suggested that a group of limited circulation products be developed for small businesses. A local commercial printer would print these products on smaller presses. Advertising pricing would be lower due to reduced costs, and distribution would be in several zones. Each zone would cover a specific area of the city where a group of businesses and their potential customers were located.

What was revealing about the task group approach was the immediate buy-in by each of the participants into finding a solution to a business challenge. From this buy-in came real problem solving and the willingness by the representative of each functional group to take recommendations back to their people and discuss how implementation could be achieved. I again think this goes back to some of the theories on human motivation. There was no carrot or threat here, only the creation of a group that provided acceptance, status, and recognition.

In the end, a very successful group of products were introduced. These products prevented the entry of marriage mail products into the market place that plagued many midsized and major metro markets.

Cross-Functional Teams at the Houston Chronicle

A cross-functional team can provide solutions to difficult market challenges. Houston was a market that was not able to ward off marriage mail. Marriage mail is a program that allows advertisers to combine their advertiser circulars in one mail package and share the mail costs. Marriage Mailers, a small direct mail operations in Los Angeles, first used the concept. . . . ADVO, a direct marketer established in 1929, bought Marriage Mailers in 1979, and began rolling out the program nationwide.

Until the introduction of marriage mail, advertising circulars were primarily distributed by newspapers and represented a very profitable revenue stream. Newspapers at the time did not feel the need to lower their rates for circular distribution because they felt they had a superior delivery system. Some retailers felt otherwise and began using the marriage mail concept, and over the next 20 years, newspapers lost the majority of grocery inserts to marriage mail.

Houston had become one of ADVO's most profitable markets to the detriment of the *Houston Post* and *Houston Chronicle*. I was charged with creating a mail product for the *Houston Chronicle* that would compete with ADVO.

Because the project would require support from across the organization, I decided to create a cross-functional team to put together a response. This team met every Friday morning for the remainder of my tenure at the *Houston Chronicle*. Within a year, we had created a product that was delivered to newspaper subscribers through the newspaper and to the remainder of the market through the U.S. Postal Service. Due to the mix of delivery, we were able to offer full market coverage at prices less than those offered by ADVO. The program was in full swing across the Houston Market in 1995, and by late 1995 all of the key retailers had abandoned ADVO and moved to the *Chronicle's* program.

The task force met each week to review the prior week's performance and address any new issues that arose. Over the following 7 years, the program, which became known as ChronDirect, was embellished to allow specific address delivery at marriage mail pricing and demographic and psycho graphic market delivery programs. The production department determined how to reduce mailing and distribution costs to ensure new entrants would not be able to match the service or the price. Today ChronDirect remains the most successful advertising distribution vehicle in the Houston market.

It is clear to me that no individual could have developed and implemented this program. It is also clear to me that cross-functional task groups can provide real employee engagement and job satisfaction while helping the organization grow.

In San Francisco, we successfully implemented the ChronDirect program, again using the cross-functional task force approach. I was able to recruit one of the key players from the Houston task group to form the task group in San Francisco. The result was a shorter lead-time for implementation of a successful program.

It has been reaffirmed time and again that the key to organizational success lies in the involvement of the workers in solutions to challenges facing the organization. The theories of hygiene and motivation factors were validated every time we found a way to get colleagues involved in problem solving. The colleagues received a sense of belonging, they received status, and sometimes they received recognition, and they felt like they had a say in the future of an organization on which they were dependent.

CHAPTER 3

Money

This chapter focuses on the need to have enough money to start an organization and then outlines different approaches to improving cash flows when needed.

Starting with Enough Money

Even the best-planned and organized effort can fail if there isn't sufficient capital to support the project through the start-up period.

First and foremost, it is critical to make certain when you start a business that there is sufficient working capital to see the company through until it can generate sufficient cash flows on its own. Any cash plan should be reviewed to ensure it is based on reality and then the cash requirements increased to account for unexpected eventualities.

Cash Requirements for New Organizations

With the *Huntsville Morning News*, a local newspaper in Huntsville, Texas, we made an assumption that key businesses would move their entire budget to the *Morning News* soon after we opened the door. It seemed reasonable because these businesses were also investors. It turned out that this assumption was incorrect, and the amount of lead-time to become a profitable business was longer than we projected and required more money than we had raised from investors.

With American Property Data, a commercial real estate venture, we had projected the right amount of lead-time and the right amount of capital that would be required. In this case, we had planned to provide start-up cash from a family oil business owned by the founders. Unfortunately, oil prices fell, and the oil business could not support American Property Data.

Harte Hanks Corporation suffered the same difficulties as the *Morning News*. The senior management of Harte Hanks orchestrated a leveraged buyout. The debt was secured by Harte Hanks properties that were located, for the most part, in the Sun Belt and were projected to have good incomes resulting from the oil-based economies. Unfortunately, the oil prices dropped shortly after the leveraged buyout, and Harte Hanks had to sell most of their properties to retire the debt incurred from the buyout.

As the above examples show, there are reasons new companies and old can find that they are short on cash. Cash crunches can impact all companies, large and small. To ensure there is adequate cash available, it is best to adopt a cash management program that is conservative. Limit debt to a minimum, find ways to free up cash from operations before borrowing, and when possible create a contingency cash fund.

The Right Business Structure

Choosing how you structure the organization can have a significant impact on its financial viability.

Changing the Structure at Health Care News

I was asked to help turn around a small regional publisher of health care newspapers. A young woman who had gained experience in community newspapers had started the newspapers. The health care news publishing business attracted a group of investors. The investors struck a deal that would allow them part ownership and would treat their investment as a loan. This of course had a significant negative impact on cash flows that resulted in serious financial shortfalls.

One of the quickest fixes for this organization was to get the investors to convert their loans to equity and eliminate the large cash flows dedicated to debt. Fortunately, the investors agreed to convert debt to equity.

Still there was a need for more cash from the investors to meet the expansion plan for the company. The key investors were three venture capital firms. Unfortunately, two of the venture capital firms had strong ties to the savings and loan industry that failed in the latter part of the

1980s. Ultimately these firms had to bow out, and we needed to find a new venture capital firm to fill the void. We did find another venture capital firm that would provide funding, but the new group did not fit well with the founding investors, and, as a result, funding did not materialize, and the whole project failed.

This particular business model might have succeeded had it had enough capital to adjust some of the marketing concepts, but the cash available simply could not support the organization. Having a better organizational structure from the beginning would have reduced unnecessary cash outflows to investors. Having a structure that attracted a larger base of investors might have reduced the impact of the Savings and Loan crisis.

Cash Flow Planning

It is important to establish a plan for paying for inventory and other expenses. Decisions need to be made regarding discounts for early payment to vendors, and it is important to understand interest costs when payments to vendors are made late.

Retailers generally have a cash flow model that allows inventory to be sold before the vendor is paid. One retailer I am familiar with pays for inventory 90 days after the goods are received from the vendor. The inventory is usually sold in 60 days.

In this situation, the retailer does not offer credit other than allowing the customer to use their credit cards, so the retailer collects the money from the sale of the inventory 30 days prior to paying the vendor. To further boost cash flows, the money due to the vendor is held in a money market account for the 30 days and earns interest.

Manufacturers, by contrast, have a cash flow model that requires payment of materials and inventory before products are sold. Here adequate start-up and operating capital is likely to be substantial and require strong banking relationships.

Debt as a funding source should be used carefully. Finding a solid lending partner and low interest rates are critical. The amount of debt required will affect overall operating costs and the ability to compete with companies that have less or no debt.

Whether due to a poor financial structure, inadequate sales, poor credit and pricing policies, too much debt, or the need to expand the business, there will be a time when additional cash is needed.

For all businesses, a periodic review of ongoing operations can yield unexpected sources of cash.

Internal Sources of Cash

For an established business, there may be opportunities to use cash within the organization for new programs.

HEB Cash Control System

The CEO of HEB Grocery Company, Charles Butt, wanted to build a new milk plant in San Antonio but did not want to borrow money. Mr. Butt felt there was enough cash flow in the 120 stores located around the state to free up the money to build a milk plant.

A senior team had been working on developing a cash management system for a couple of years but had not come up with a system that could be implemented successfully. Most of the approaches centered on the frequent harvesting of cash from registers in the stores and sending the cash to the local banks. The corporate office would then collect the cash from the various banks. What made the system impractical was the inability to accurately predict the amount of money each store would request for the next day's operation. Even if cash were harvested hourly from the stores, the managers might request an amount equal to or greater the next day for store operations. Stores needed cash to buy local inventory and cash customer's checks. Store managers did not want to disappoint customers or be unable to purchase local inventory items when they were needed and in many cases requested ample amounts of cash to ensure they could serve their customers.[1]

It occurred to me that corporate managers should not be involved in managing the cash at the store level. I gave it some thought and proposed a system that treated money requested by store managers as a loan from the corporate office.[2] We established the loan rate as the same as charged by a bank. Store managers were told they could withdraw as much as they felt they needed without any interest charge as long as the money was efficiently used. Efficient use meant that if all of the money requested above the established target for the store were converted to inventory or checks, there would be no interest charge. Formulas were developed that would adjust the cash withdrawal limit for each store based on the efficient use of cash.

Each store's withdrawal and deposit history was analyzed and was the basis for setting withdrawal targets for the store managers. If a store requested more than the withdrawal target for the store and redeposited cash, this excess cash was considered inefficiently used and received a penalty or interest charge. These interest or penalty charges were considered part of the store's operating costs and affected store managers' annual bonuses.

This approach involved store managers in controlling cash throughout the system and focused on the efficient use of cash. The system, once implemented, freed up $1 million in 6 weeks.

HEB, at that time, had no reporting mechanisms that measured the amount of cash that could be freed up or how well cash was managed on a daily basis. After addressing the need for cash and developing the system, a cash efficiency reporting system was created.

Assets Written Off as a Source of Cash

As companies write off assets assumed to be of little value, there may be an opportunity to convert these "lost" assets to cash if managers are reminded that a write-off does not mean they cease to exist.

Operating cash flows are generated from a company's sales. Most companies find that sales can be increased when they offer credit terms to their customers. It is critical in the planning stages to determine the type of credit that will increase sales and provide solid cash flows. It is also important to have quality tracking and collection efforts when customers fail to pay for products and services purchased on credit.

Accounts Receivable at the Caller-Times

Harte Hanks Corporation owned the *Corpus Christi Caller-Times* at a time when the corporate focus was on rapid company growth, and accurate financial reporting and asset management was crucial. The *Caller-Times* was the flagship of the corporation and a focus of attention. After joining the corporation I was asked to manage the accounting and credit divisions at the *Caller-Times*.

In an effort to clean up the physical appearance of the accounting area, I asked that a room full of old invoices be moved out and destroyed. As we were moving the invoices to trash, I noticed that many of them were several years old. I asked an accounting manager why we would hold on to invoices for such a long time. He replied that the invoices were still owed but there had been no success in collecting them and had subsequently been written off as bad debt.

We decided to turn them over to a collection agency. The fees were high, up to 30% of the amount collected, but would yield significant amounts of cash if collected. Over the next 6 months, almost all of the invoices were collected, and a significant amount of cash was added to the company's coffers.

In addition, a new program was implemented that focused on collecting old accounts. As invoices were written off as uncollectible, they were logged into a credit collection system before being turned over to the collection agency.

At the *Corpus Christi Caller-Times*, there was no balance sheet account that indicated a set of old invoices existed that were of some value. This is because corporations usually create a reserve for bad debt after an invoice is 60 to 90 days old. During this period, the amount of uncollected invoices remains on the balance sheet. After the invoices remain uncollected for an additional period of time, corporations usually write them off as uncollectible. When they are written off, they are no longer on the balance sheet and managers do not spend a lot of time focusing on these invoices. After the new program was implemented at the *Caller-Times*, a reporting system was created that kept managers apprised of the potential cash available in old invoices.

Cash in Crises

Even in the direst situations, actions can be taken that create cash flows to sustain an organization.

Saving the Conroe Morning News

Monte Hawthorne, who owned the *Conroe Morning News* in Conroe, Texas, contacted me. Monte and an investor group had started the *Conroe Morning News* to compete with the *Conroe Courier*. The *Courier* had been the primary paper for Conroe, Texas, since 1896 and had a strong advertising base.

The Morning News had been started in 1984 and had not been able to gain a market share large enough to support the newspaper operations. When Monte called me, he indicated that the investor group had grown tired of covering cash shortfalls.

I agreed to help. I spent a few days looking at the financial history and meeting with the managers to get a feel for the operations. After reviewing the details, it was clear that drastic action would have to be taken to save the organization.

The first order of the day was to increase ad rates significantly (17%). With this announcement, there was considerable concern from the sales force. I knew the rate increase was substantial, but I also knew that there had been several major changes in the newspaper over the past year. In reviewing the records, it looked like none of the changes made by management had affected the core customers' ad volumes. It was also clear that the *Conroe Morning News* charged less than the competition and that the rate increase would still leave it with a competitive edge.

Beyond the rate increase, there was a backlog of bills due to vendors. The material provided by the vendors was critical to continued operations as was their goodwill.

For this challenge, I used the "hammer down" process. I met with vendors and asked them to forgive an amount of the past due. In some cases I was able to get the past due amount reduced by 90%. The approach was simple. I told the vendors that the alternative was to write off the entire amount because the *Conroe Morning News* would no longer be in business. This was the truth, and the vendors accepted the terms that would allow us to survive.

Once we had established a new amount that was past due, I asked the vendors to allow us to pay down the past due amounts over time. Again this was difficult for the vendors to accept, but there was no alternative.

So we began paying down the past due amounts while paying for the full amount due on new supplies when they were received.

Fortunately all of the actions taken were successful. Advertising revenues increased by the full 17%, which provided a profit. The reworking of past due amounts with vendors reduced cash outflows enough that the *Conroe Morning News* was able to stay in business. The turnaround took about 6 weeks.

We eventually sold the *Morning News* to the *Courier*, which allowed the *Morning News* investors to recoup their investment and allowed the *Courier* to continue serving the market.

This approach for a financial turnaround was used again when I was approached to help a small ethnic newspaper (The *Jewish Herald-Voice*) that was facing the prospect of going out of business due to the sharp downturn in business caused by the recent recession.

After reviewing the financial records, we determined that by changing to a different type of newsprint, printing costs could be reduced by 33%. In addition, we found that rates could be raised even in the midst of a recession. Finally, we worked with vendors to restructure payments for past due amounts. Again the results were positive, and in about 6 weeks the *Herald-Voice* was on solid financial ground.

It is clear that an organization must have an adequate supply of money to stay in business and to grow to its potential. The good news is that with good planning, adequate cash can be made available, and even when unexpected business changes impact cash levels negatively, there are programs that can produce needed cash to continue operations.

CHAPTER 4

Methods

Methods describe the design of how an organization will perform the activities required by a business plan. The following are examples of how companies were organized to match the business plan.

Organizational Structure

Typically an organization is set up according to function. There is usually a grouping of functions that report to the chief operating officer. The most common groupings are as follows:

1. Finance for accounting, credit, financial assets, and financial reporting
2. Production for manufacturing, assembly, and product packaging
3. Marketing for advertising, internal and external communication, media planning, and market research
4. Administration for human resources, facility maintenance, benefits, real estate, security, equipment, and infrastructure
5. Information technology for computer hardware and software and support technology (telephones, networks, some production equipment)
6. Distribution for logistics, inventory planning, and execution
7. Sales for serving the customer base and opening new markets

When organizations are very small, the functions may not be formally identified, and just a few individuals may manage all functions. As organizations grow in size and complexity, each of these functions will likely have a manager and separate staff.

Corpus Christi Caller-Times Information Flow

Understanding the flow of information in an organization can help design an efficient and effective organizational structure.

The general manager of the *Caller-Times*, asked me to review the organization to see if there might be a way of improving the organization's efficiency and effectiveness. Over the years, the organization had added new functions and, rather than having them absorbed by the existing departmental functions, they reported directly to the general manager. The resulting structure required the general manager to focus most of his management time on internal management questions. This reduced his ability to focus on changing market needs and developing new market strategies.

For the analysis, we looked at the types of information that were needed by management and what departments provided the information. I separated the information management needed into three broad categories:

1. Information required for long-term success
2. Information on customer satisfaction
3. Information on profitability

We analyzed the information based on which organizational function provided the information and whether the information was sent to management or other departments. We then determined the types of information that could be combined by putting the reporting entities in the same functional areas and perhaps combining reporting mechanisms.

After a review, we were able to create an administrative management department with a manager who reported directly to the general manager. In addition, we were able to take several functions and merge them with existing departments. To merge departments, we analyzed the type of information handled by each function and combined groups that created or handled similar information. This analysis uncovered areas of duplication of effort that were eliminated.

The result of the organizational analysis was the reduction of those reporting directly to the general manager from 10 to 5 managers. There was also a significant improvement in the quality of the information being generated and a reduction in the quantity of reporting.

Huntsville Morning News Work Flow

Setting up workflow in an organization is as critical to its success as having adequate resources and organizational structure.

When we started the *Huntsville Morning News*, not only did we need a plan that allowed the creation of facilities, production capabilities, and a staff within a 90-day window, we also needed to be organized in a fashion that would allow us to produce a high quality product at a very low operating cost.

To accomplish this, we had to review every step in creating a newspaper and analyze workflows. We needed to lay out the work area in a way that allowed work to flow smoothly and eliminate barriers. As part of the planning process, we worked with the building contractors and equipment vendors to create the most efficient organization possible.

The building was designed so that advertising was next to the accounting department, which allowed ads to be accounted for and invoices mailed quickly. The ads flowed directly into the area that designed the daily newspaper (ads were placed first in the design and editorial content followed). The newspaper design group and the editorial group were arranged so that editorial and ad copy flowed directly to the composing area where the newspaper was actually assembled.

The composing area was arranged to allow the final version of pages for the newspaper to flow directly to the press operations. Finally, the press and newspaper assembly areas were located next to the dock to allow rapid movement of the newspaper to the people who distributed the newspaper. The result of close attention to how we organized allowed us to produce a newspaper with about half the staff of similar-sized newspapers at the time.

American Property Data Information Flow

Employing methods and technology that govern the interaction of people and information in the most productive fashion can be critical to succeeding as a business.

Andy Schoepf contacted me and asked me to help him and his brothers, Beryl and George, start a new type of commercial real estate brokerage service. The commercial real estate service was intriguing. The idea was to collect real estate information on properties available throughout the United States and create a database that could be used by real estate brokers and investors.

I did the programming of the system using an off-the-shelf database program. This allowed properties to be entered into a database and then be queried on characteristics in which various buyers would be interested.

Once I was certain the software would perform as required, we set out to create an organization that would collect property data and market the product.

The first step would be to attract major commercial real estate brokers in key markets around the country to participate by entering their property listings in the system. Simultaneously, we would sell the listing service to key real estate buyers such as pension funds and real estate investment trusts.

Within a few weeks, we sold the concept to several brokers and real estate investment groups. The commercial brokers were given an exclusive territory to represent American Property Data (APD) and paid a fee for that privilege. These brokers were able to attract listings more effectively because they could quickly market properties to buyers nationwide.

Investors simply subscribed to the service and received data on new properties as they were entered into the system. When they found properties matching their investment parameters, they would request a full information packet. Once requested, a full information packet with color photos would be sent via express mail.

Clearly, to be successful, APD had to collect data from the commercial brokers and make the data available to buyers quickly. The amount of data flowing to and from buyers made it necessary to employ computer-generated data exchange.

To solve the potential problems of format and computer compatibility, APD provided computers with the software downloaded to both brokers and investors as part of the system. Brokers would download new properties daily. Periodically, all buyers' and brokers' computers would be refreshed with updated data.

Sales to investors required the ability to sell the value of a national database of commercial property. For this, we established a telephone sales department comprising individuals with commercial sales agent experience.

Sales to commercial real estate brokers would require the ability to demonstrate the value of being an exclusive representative for APD and the value of entering the brokers' listings into a national database. To convince commercial brokers to participate would require sales people who fully understood the system and real estate brokerage. Because APD wanted to attract the top broker in a market, the APD salesperson needed to be experienced and an executive of the company. We were able to recruit an individual who had been a senior broker for a national commercial real estate firm to handle broker sales.

APD grew in two years to 60 broker offices nationwide with a property inventory of over $2 billion. This was accomplished with a staff of about 12 people in our Houston office.

We eventually sold APD to one of the first brokers to join the system, and he transformed it into a commercial real estate auction program.

Building a Network of Independent Businesses

Utilizing a network of businesses as partners can provide instant access to multiple markets while providing consistency on sales approaches and customer support.

Recently my business partner and I identified an opportunity to capitalize on the growth of the Chinese manufacturing capabilities and the new growing LED display market. My business partner and I traveled to China to find and purchase an interest in an LED-manufacturing facility.

We made several trips to China and visited LED manufacturers in several cities before finally deciding to invest in a manufacturer in Beijing. After making the investment, the Chinese shareholders elected to change their company's name to GW LEDS, the same name that we had chosen for our company in the United States that would market the signs.

There was a strong demand for LED signs in the United States, and there were reputable U.S. manufacturers. We felt that we could offer a lower-priced, high-quality sign and create a solid business. Because our competition guaranteed their product's quality and provided support services, we felt that we had to do the same.

To develop the U.S. market, we established a network of authorized brokers that would sell, install, and service the GW LEDS signs. We chose brokers that had their own sign company and a good reputation. Their affiliation with GW LEDS would allow them to add LED signs to their product line.

These brokers were trained at our offices in Houston. For training sessions, we used a large LED screen tied to the Internet and connected with our technicians in Beijing using Skype. This kept our training costs to a bare minimum and the quality of training at the highest level possible by being able to allow brokers to have questions answered by technicians and software engineers building the systems. When the training was complete, these brokers went back to their markets and began selling the product.

The sign industry is pretty much a cash business. When a sign is sold a down payment is made (usually 50%), and when the sign is installed the final payment is made. Because we owned a significant share of the factory, we were able to arrange payments for the signs in the same manner as the customers paid for them. So, from the outset, there was a positive cash flow from sales.

This organizational design allowed us to rely on the expertise of the factory to hold down the cost, the expertise of the broker to sell and service the signs and the use of industry norms to create a positive cash flow.

What did not work was the difficulty in updating new technology in the signs that had been sold. The distance and language difficulties made it difficult to compete with firms whose manufacturing and service arms were in the United States. To compete directly for the U.S. market, we would have had to move a service group to the United States, and this cost would have caused us to raise prices to levels that were no longer advantageous.

We ultimately sold our positions in this company, which is still manufacturing LED signs for Asia and some parts of Europe.

Organizational Strategy for Disruptive Innovations

Understanding the nature of an innovation can determine the organizational structure and methods that will be most successful.

I was invited by Harvard's Clay Christensen to be on a panel at a conference hosted by Christensen and George Gilder. The panel would be discussing disruptive innovations that were impacting the newspaper industry. The Internet was having a significant impact on the industry.

The conference was a 3-day program, and the attendees were investors and businesspeople looking for the next big investment opportunity. For my part, I told the crowd that I felt like newspapers were likely to survive the Internet and that the new technologies were more of a sustaining technology than a disruptive innovation.

It has taken several years to really try to understand what the Internet has done to the newspaper industry and to try to make sense of how newspapers reacted to the challenge.

Basically, the disruptive innovation theories say that disruptive innovations are likely to occur when industries continue to improve their products at a faster rate than the new improvements can be found useful by a meaningful segment of the customer base. This allows a new company to come in with a "good-enough" product at a lower price that attracts the least profitable customers. Over time, the new company (the disruptor) improves its products and takes more and more of the industry leader's customers. The customers attracted by the disruptor are usually the least profitable for the industry leader because they do not need all the product attributes offered and will accept a good-enough replacement for a lower price.

These theories also introduce the concept of a sustaining innovation. A sustaining innovation allows the industry leaders to better serve their customers.

Throughout the theories, it is noted that the structure of an organization can prevent an industry leader from successfully competing against an industry entrant with a disruptive innovation. One primary reason is the industry leader's most profitable customers' demands prevent a focus on innovations targeting their least profitable customers. Clay suggests the industry leader should spin-off an organization solely focused on competing in the realm of the disruptive innovation.

For a sustaining innovation, a spin-off company is not recommended because the innovation is intended to improve the ability to serve the needs of the current customer base.

A final point for consideration is the thought that businesses should not focus on the customer but rather the job the customer is "hiring" the company's product to perform.

With this basic description of disruptive and sustaining innovations, it is interesting to consider the impact of the Internet on the newspaper business and how the newspaper industry reacted. More importantly, I think there are answers for how newspapers can move forward and how they might have prevented the severity of the financial impact on the industry. Finally, I think that other industries may be able to use these lessons to improve success in both the disruptive and sustaining innovation categories.

First consider the impact of the Internet on the newspaper industry:

1. It allowed the very profitable classified business to move quickly to technologically advanced format.
2. It allowed the newspaper's largest, most profitable customers to better segment and target their customers by linking to word searches.
3. It allowed smaller advertisers (not necessarily less profitable customers) to rotate digital ads at a lower price than newspapers (not necessarily a lower cost per customer reached).

This does not suggest that newspapers had improved their products beyond the levels needed by their customers. Rather, it suggests that there were pent-up demands by customers who were waiting for a new platform that better performed the jobs they needed done.

As the Internet's impact on the newspaper has increased, so have the programs to serve its users. Social networking, social gaming programs, and interactive entertainment are attracting huge audiences. These are all new programs that could not be performed by newspapers but were wanted by newspaper customers.

The Internet was and is a sustaining innovation. That is, if each and every innovation mentioned above had been introduced by the newspaper industry, the customer base from least profitable to most profitable would have quickly adopted the programs.

This can be verified because almost all newspaper customers quickly adopted or experimented with those programs. Facebook, Twitter, and similar programs allow networks to share news as it happens. LinkedIn allows professionals to stay networked. Interactive games allow entertainment platforms that include multiple players. All of these programs and a growing number daily could have been under the umbrella of newspapers' products.

So why did newspapers miss the boat? Interestingly, newspapers acted as though the Internet was a game changer. Most newspapers set up a separate organization to operate their website. Most of those remain as a separate entity today. These new organizations created their own programming, content, and ad programs.

Unfortunately, because they were a separate organization, they began to compete with the newspaper and began converting newspaper programs to a website. They did not look at new ways to serve current newspaper customers, rather they looked at new ways to present the newspaper digitally to the market. Some saw the newspaper website as a means of reaching newspaper readers who had been lost or reaching new markets. This approach led to reformatting traditional news stories, entertainment, and advertising.

To jump-start the advertising, the newspaper website was given a share of the print revenue. This unfortunately had the impact of making it difficult to determine the success of the website programs.

In other words, newspapers treated the Internet and the products as disruptive innovations when in fact they were sustaining innovations. A corollary to the organizational structure for disruptive innovations is that by treating a sustaining technology as a disruptive technology and creating a separate structure, the industry leader impedes its own ability to serve its customers and opens opportunities for competitors to enter the market. I believe this is what happened to the newspaper industry.

It appears that if there had been a litmus test that could have categorized the Internet as a sustaining technology, the outcome might have been different. If the Internet had been defined as a sustaining innovation, the organization would have structured the Internet components as part of the current organization. For example, the web-based innovations for classified advertising would have been structured as part of the advertising department. Rather than determining ways to add on classified newspaper ads to the newspaper website, newspapers might have been the ones to create interactive searches for their classified customers. Instead, they found themselves reacting to innovators outside of the industry and giving away any value they might have retained.

The ability to update stories might have provided marketing assistance for the circulation department. Interactive updates might have been the invention of newspapers had the newsroom had the responsibility for the digital news projects.

Clearly, there would have been no organization using newspaper resources and competing directly with the newspaper—a structure that should only be used with disruptive innovations.

Unfortunately at the time, the theories of disruptive and sustaining innovations were new and there was not a widely accepted process for identifying innovation types and relating them to organizational structures.

What should newspapers do now? They should begin integrating the web functions with the newspaper. It should not be a separate entity. Begin finding ways to understand the jobs advertisers and readers are hiring newspapers to do and use all of the technologies to create a symbiotic array of products to do those jobs.

The *Houston Business Journal* for example, a weekly paid subscription product targeting business executives, has found a way of building on its print product by using new technologies. First, it introduced the digital version of the print product and began marketing bulk subscriptions to businesses, which provided a digital copy for each of the subscribing company's executives. The journal then provided a daily email to these executives updating local business activities through a link to their website. Here the *Houston Business Journal* clearly understood the job that needed to be done was to make business executives more effective in the Houston market and went about doing that job in a way that was meaningful to executives and created a business opportunity for *Houston Business Journal*.

What should industries do in the future? First they should identify the jobs that a new innovation does for the consumers. If it does the same jobs that the industry performs but with greater efficacy and offers product attributes previously unavailable then the innovation should be classified as a sustaining innovation. Why is this sustaining? Because by adding the innovation the current leader improves its ability to serve its best customers better.

If the new innovation does the same jobs but does so at a lower cost with a "good enough" product that offers no new capabilities then it should be classified as a disruptive innovation. Why is this disruptive? Because by adding the innovation, the current leader would have to change its business model to compete for its least profitable customers. To be proactive, it is better to add a separate organization that focuses only on that market or that innovation.

CHAPTER 5

Directing

Activating Resources

Directing is the management method of activating resources once the plan is finalized and the resources are organized to carry out the plan.

In large part, directing involves giving instructions to individuals who do the actual work. While this is closely related to the evaluating tasks and setting standards, it differs in the sense that it is a dynamic process whereas Standards of Performance are fixed or static for a period of time.

Cross-Functional Teams to Direct Activities

To create an environment that focuses on achievement of organizational goals, it is necessary to make certain all individuals are "in the loop." There is nothing that sets a company back more rapidly than an employee or group of employees who are not synchronized with the rest of the organization.

Consider the *Houston Chronicle*. We had made great strides in growing ad revenues and circulation. We felt like continued growth would be based on closer relationships with our advertisers and our subscribers.

We were also a very big company, and it was at times difficult to get everyone on the "same page." The production or manufacturing side of the business had shown great success in providing the ability to move massive amounts of advertising and editorial information through systems that created the daily newspaper. The production group also felt that it was important to keep workflows within established processes. Thus, there were limitations on the ability to customize products for our customers.

The marketplace our advertisers competed in required the most sophisticated customized marketing strategies available. Increasingly, it looked like small advertising companies with great flexibility were going to be able to outmaneuver the *Chronicle.*

The *Chronicle*'s New Product Task Group used a cross-functional task group to determine how best to direct the organization's resources to meet customer's needs. It was the manufacturing side of the business that sought production control and process uniformity that was at odds with the sales division that needed the ability to customize products. As the New Product Task Group studied these competing goals, solutions were developed that met the needs of the manufacturing and the sales side of the organization.

It was the manufacturing participants who were able to figure out how to customize products while still producing large enough volumes to make the operation profitable.

The sales participants not only described the customers' needs but also, through the process, designed sales programs that supported the manufacturing solutions.

The accounting division found ways of pricing that ensured profitability and allowed customers to purchase ad packages suited to their needs. The computer group devised methods of segmenting the market for customer demanded ad campaigns that fit with the manufacturing capabilities and sales' needs.

Once products were finalized, all participants understood how the project was to work and how each group was to contribute. The implementation was self-directed by each department manager, and the overall direction was reviewed weekly by the New Products Task Group.

Metrics were established for each area of responsibility and the weekly reviews were used to reallocate resources and efforts to keep the project on a successful track.

The *Houston Chronicle*'s New Products Task Group took the lead in indentifying market needs and developing new product strategies. Products introduced included a weekly entertainment and dining guide, distribution programs for third-party publications, customized printing and distribution programs, and direct mail programs.

In San Francisco, a similar New Products Task Group introduced a weekly food and wine section, revamped the Sunday entertainment section, created new online products, and developed a series of wine and food competitions.

Desert Storm—Adjusting to Changing Needs

For organizations to have the highest levels of success, it is critical that planning and organizing are supported by the daily direction and deployment of resources.

If the human resources are acting in concert it is important to have all other resources deployed with the same discipline. Cash must be available when needed, manufacturing must have equipment capacity that matches demand, marketing campaigns must support sales and manufacturing programs, and so on.

One of the best examples of directing resources to ensure a successful outcome was the U.S. military's deployment of resources to support the 1990-1991 Persian Gulf War. This was the largest rapid movement of troops and supplies ever undertaken by the U.S. military.

The following excerpt is from a report prepared by Donna Heivilin, Director, Logistic Issues, and U.S. Comptrollers Office. The report demonstrates both the importance of resource deployment and the ability of the military to succeed in the most difficult situations.

Executive Summary

Purpose

Operations *Desert Shield* and *Desert Storm* involved the largest rapid movement of troops and supplies ever undertaken by the U.S. military. The Chairman, Subcommittee on Oversight of Government Management, Senate Committee on Governmental Affairs, asked GAO to report on the Department of Defense's (DoD) efforts to supply troops deployed to *Desert Shield/Storm* with necessary support items and repair parts.

GAO'S objectives were to summarize how DOD'S *logistics* system supplied:

The land-based forces (GAO did not include navy units or sea-based marine corps units) and to obtain observations on *logistics* support from military officials who had been involved in *Desert Shield* and *Desert Storm*. GAO sent a team to Saudi Arabia and Bahrain in April 1991 to gather these first-hand observations.

(*Continued*)

(*Continued*)

Background

Desert Shield, the protection of Saudi Arabia from Iraqi aggression and of U.S. vital interests, began on August 7, 1990, with the deployment of U.S. troops to Saudi Arabia. *Desert Storm*, the liberating of Kuwait, began on January 17,1991, with the commencement of the air campaign; the ground campaign began on February 24, 1991. Both the ground and air campaigns ended on February 28, 1991.

DOD undertook a massive logistical task to transport, receive, and sustain a force of over 500,000 troops while overcoming tremendous distances, harsh *desert* environment, and the absence of U.S. military troops stationed in Saudi Arabia. Also, logistical support difficulties were created by national policy and command decisions to (1) initially deploy combat forces in advance of support units, (2) revise mission requirements for some of the U.S. weapons systems, and (3) deploy certain new weapon systems without their full complement of spare parts and support material. Because of the short period of hostilities, *Desert Shield/Storm* did not test the supply system's ability to sustain a protracted campaign.

Results in Brief

The U.S. military's ability to move massive amounts of troops and material for *Desert Shield/Storm* was a significant achievement. As might be expected of such a huge and complex undertaking, however, not all went smoothly. GAO obtained observations from U.S. military personnel in the United States and in Saudi Arabia and Bahrain on what lessons could be learned to both avoid future occurrences of logistical problems and replicate the management practices and ingenuity U.S. military personnel used to overcome many of these problems.

Executive Summary

Personnel in *Desert Shield/Storm* were able to maintain high readiness rates despite situations such as missing information on location and unit distribution of parts and supplies, transportation delays, and use of newly fielded weapons systems. Personnel used flexibility and ingenuity to meet the needs and maintain readiness. For example, critical parts were obtained by stripping inoperable equipment, trading with like units, and purchasing from the local economy.

DOD was able to adequately provide food and clothing to U.S. troops deployed to *Desert Shield/Storm*. Food and clothing can be significant morale factors in locations far from home, and some improvements are possible in terms of variety and quality of meals available to the Army and the Marine Corps and availability of *desert* uniforms and boots to personnel. The Army is reevaluating its feeding plan because of some of the shortfalls and inadequate industrial base response to increased requirements. While all troops obtained military clothing and chemical ensembles, not all received the proper size or the required types or amounts.

Prepositioning of supplies by the Air Force and the Marines was considered to be successful in achieving the rapid deployment of supplies to Saudi Arabia. In the Marine Corps, in some instances, supplies that had been predesignated for one unit were reallocated to other units (based on commander's decisions). The Marine Corps also had problems with the management of prepositioned supplies that were not used for *Desert Shield/Storm* missions.

Principal Findings

Repair Parts

Air Force personnel at units GAO visited said that they never missed a mission because of a shortage of repair parts, readiness rates of aircraft during *Desert Shield/Storm* averaged 93% for Air Force aircraft and ranged from 90% to 97% for selected Army equipment during *Desert Storm*, according to Air Force and Army Central Command statistics. The Marine Corps units GAO visited estimated overall readiness rates ranging from 90% to 95%. The Army, the Air Force, and the Marines all had supply lists/prepackaged kits with the repair parts and supplies essential to support and sustain combat until the supply system

(*Continued*)

(Continued)

adjusted to the increased demand. To obtain the high unit readiness rates, these lists/kits were supplemented. *Desert Shield/Storm* personnel interviewed by GAO made observations on how to better tailor these supplies to wartime needs. All the units GAO visited described how they used intensive management, flexibility, and ingenuity to ensure that parts were obtained in a timely manner and high readiness rates were maintained. These efforts included obtaining parts from other units, rebuilding and reusing parts, buying parts and repair services on the local economy, taking parts from nonmission capable equipment, and managing transportation intensively to help lessen delays in obtaining needed parts.

The Army was able to maintain high readiness rates in part because of the high priority given to supplying parts to units, but it did not have visibility of repair parts at the unit levels in the Persian Gulf and thus could not readily redistribute parts among units. With the Marine Corps' initial priority of rapidly unloading the Marine Prepositioning Force ships to support the deployment of combat troops in August 1990, the Corps experienced some difficulty controlling inventories of repair parts. A Marine Corps headquarters official said this was due to a Central Command decision to send combat forces before support personnel.

The Air Force directly addressed inventory problems, and by January 1991, it had a central computer system operating that provided spare parts visibility.

In addition, GAO was told of some instances of the inefficient use of the priority system for ordering repair parts and how some units overcame problems in obtaining needed parts for a communications unit and for newly fielded systems.

Food and Clothing

Due to restrictions from the host nation's cultural and religious practices, the provision of food and clothing was a very important factor in maintaining the morale of *Desert Shield/Storm* personnel.

Although each military service had a field feeding plan, the type and variety of food depended on the units' locations. For example, the Air Force, with fixed locations, had more fresh food available than the mobile Army and Marine units that used more packaged rations. All three services received significant contributions of fresh food from the host nation. The Air Force's and the Marine Corps' feeding plans were met or exceeded during the operation. While the Army was not able to meet its feeding plan for all units, it did introduce a morale booster, the "wolfmobiles," which served hamburgers, hot dogs, and french fries. Army and Marine Corps units GAO visited verified the reported complaints about the quality and lack of variety in some of the meals served. A Marine Corps headquarters official attributed this to the tactical situation. Personnel GAO talked to had uniforms, boots, and chemical gear, but there were some problems with the availability of sizes and amounts. Also, *desert* camouflage uniforms and *desert* boots were not always available, especially for Air Force personnel.

Other Desert Shield/Storm, The Marine Corps' Maritime Prepositioning Force, and the Air Force's Logistics Issues

Harvest Falcon prepositioning program was successful in both expediting the deployment of supplies and support equipment to Saudi Arabia. The Marines, however, did experience distribution and inventory problems due to the tactical situation.

GAO obtained information on a number of other supply issues, including needed items purchased outside the supply system in the United States for deploying units and by units in Saudi Arabia. Items were purchased before deployment because the items were not in the supply system or could be obtained sooner. Units purchased needed supplies and services such as food, potable water, fuel, and heavy transportation equipment in Saudi Arabia because (1) specific items were not available in the supply system; (2) it reduced the burden on the transportation system, both from the United States and in theater; and (3) the supplies were obtained sooner.

(*Continued*)

(Continued)

Recommendations

GAO is presenting observations of U.S. military personnel and is not making recommendations.

Agency Comments

GAO obtained oral comments on a draft of this report from DOD and incorporated them, where applicable. DOD generally agreed with the issues raised in this report GAO/NSIAD-92-26 *Desert Shield/ Storm Logistics.*

CHAPTER 6

Controls

Controls are systems that allow managers to assess how well an organization is performing when compared with the plan. The most used control systems are the budgeting and financial reporting systems. As I have noted, a budget is the quantification of the plan. The better thought-out and detailed the plan, the better the budget.

If a plan calls for the opening of a new store in March and the construction takes three months, then the budget for January would show an increase in construction-related expenses and in April would show revenue related to the new store opening.

In most companies, managers report how well their departments are performing vis-à-vis the plan and budget. In the previous example, if construction costs are below the budget, it could be a good thing in that the managers are holding construction costs down, or it could be a bad thing where the project has fallen behind schedule.

Many companies require managers to report only major variances from the plan and that is usually done on a monthly basis. For companies that operate in more volatile and time-sensitive environments, managers must report budget variances more frequently.

Tracking and Adjusting to Reach Budgeted Goals

The Caller-Times System

At the *Corpus Christi Caller-Times*, we developed a system that broke the annual plan down into weekly budgets for each operating area. Each week, the operating managers met with the general manager to discuss how the performance was compared with the plan and budget for the week and how any variances might impact the company's ability to reach monthly and ultimately annual goals.

This system was used throughout Harte Hanks and allowed the CEO to manage the company more effectively. It was not unusual for a variance to be reported that would have a negative impact on overall performance. The ability to report on a weekly basis allowed adjustments from areas performing better than plan to offset negative variances.

This weekly reporting focused almost entirely on financial performance. This is appropriate because a firm that is not performing well financially will not be able to survive for the long term. So it is possible that nonfinancial programs that are deemed important for long-term success may be canceled or delayed to meet short-term financial goals.

The weekly variance reporting system at the *Caller-Times* allowed the company to better meet its financial goals and to note where nonfinancial goals were being delayed or canceled. Thus, if there was a key nonfinancial goal that was being delayed, it gave key managers the ability to find funding for the project.

Using Technology to Improve Tracking at the *Houston Chronicle*

The *Houston Chronicle*'s CFO, Rick Winegarden and CIO, Susan Shows developed a financial reporting system that allowed managers to compare their performance to the plan and budget on a daily basis. The financial system at the *Chronicle* collected data from all departments continually. This data constantly updated accounting, inventory, manufacturing, and sales reporting systems.

At both the *Caller-Times* and the *Chronicle*, managers were able to project a month or so in advance based on the information they were provided. This ability led to improved financial performance and a better understanding by managers of the annual plan and budget.

Using Controls for a Successful Start-Up

Controls can provide information that helps meet the organization's goals.

Controls at American Property Data

With a small start-up company like American Property Data (APD), control systems were crucial. Resources were limited, and the concept was new. Every program initiated had to be tracked to make certain resources were not wasted and that the programs performed as expected.

For resource utilization, we used systems similar to those used at the *Caller-Times* along with budgets that were tied to financial reporting systems.

In addition, APD used daily tracking sheets and control logs to ensure investors received packages that were ordered and to ensure the property inventory was accurate. If packages were not delivered or if the information was inaccurate, the credibility of the organization would have been in question in an industry that depended on the efficient flow of accurate information.

Reporting Accuracy

It is critical that control systems report performance accurately to ensure quality information for making decisions.

The Caller-Times Accounts Payable Process

At the *Caller-Times*, we found that some managers would hold onto invoices until payment would fit into the approved budget. This had the effect of misstating real performance and in some cases increased cost by adding late charges or missing early payment discounts.

A simple system that alerted vendors to send all invoices to the accounts payable office was implemented. The Accounts Payable Clerk would log in the invoices and forward them to the responsible manager for approval. Due dates were recorded when the invoice was logged in. The accounts payable clerk would review the log daily and follow up with managers to make certain the bills were approved for payment within the needed timeline.

The accounts payable system also provided access to all invoices by the financial system assuring that expenses were recorded in the proper time frame.

Using Technology for Inventory Control

Inventory is usually one of the biggest assets, and quality inventory controls can improve cash flows and reduce operating costs.

HEB Inventory Tracking System

HEB Grocery Company uses electronic scanning registers in its stores. The registers not only provide the ability to offer quicker and more accurate customer service at the customer check-out but also the opportunity for better inventory controls.

The grocery business is usually a low-profit margin business and maximizing inventory turns while minimizing inventory costs is essential. The new electronic registers allow major improvements in managing inventories.

As part of an inventory control project, each product was studied to determine a safety stock level. Safety stock is the stock that must be on hand to last until new stock arrives. Before the advent of electronic registers, stock managers determined the amount they kept in stock while waiting on a new delivery. This was a subjective judgment based on the stock manager's experience. Using this approach, out-of-stock and overstock conditions were commonplace.

HEB was one of the first to use the electronic registers to improve inventory management. These registers were included in the computer network that tracked inventory. As a result, as merchandise is recorded as sold, it is deducted from inventory, and when the store inventory reaches a reorder point, merchandise is ordered. This tracking allows the ability to better predict inventory requirements at store levels.

Better control of inventory not only helps manage the inventory and cash, it helps manage the utilization of the trucking system that supplies the stores and construction costs associated with inventory space at the store level.

Credit Controls for Organizational Health

Controlling the amount of credit available to customers and continually reviewing the customers' debt levels and payment history can assure the company's financial health. Dealing with problem accounts requires special attention.

Sales revenue is the lifeblood of an organization. Credit is a means of allowing customers to buy according to their cash flows. As long as the customers' cash flows allow the retirement of the debt extended to them, the wheels of commerce turn smoothly.

When establishing credit for a customer, it is important that a formal financial review is performed. This allows an indication of the customer's ability and promptness in paying their bills.

After approving customers for credit, a control system should be established that tracks the days in receivable for each customer and the available credit for each customer. When the amount in receivables or the time in receivables reaches a pre-established limit, the sales managers responsible for the account are notified.

It is usually best for the sales manager to visit with the customer to determine whether there is a developing problem rather than having a credit limit that automatically stops available credit. This prevents stopping credit to a good customer with a short-term cash flow challenge. For example, a customer who is experiencing a significant increase in business but is waiting for cash from the new business. In these instances, a review of the customer's credit might increase the credit limit.

There will be cases when the sales manager reports back to the credit department that a customer is having financial difficulties. In these cases, it may be necessary to limit or eliminate credit availability. It may also represent an opportunity to develop a program to help the customer through a difficult time.

Standards of Performance as a Control System

In all areas of control, it is important to understand that employees are involved in successful execution. Well thought-out "Standards of Performance" can be a significant tool for providing quality control for the operation. For example, accumulating data for days in accounts receivable, inventory turns, or cash balances provide metrics to set standards and specific goals for individuals to achieve success. When the standards reflect success requirements of the organization, the cumulative success of individuals yields success for the organization.

PART II

Marketing

This section of the book focuses on the principles of marketing. For established businesses, this section of the book will provide tools that will allow the business to protect and grow its position in the market. For new businesses, this section of the book will provide the steps required to analyze customer segments, evaluate the market size, and clarify the overall approach to the market.

CHAPTER 7

Products and Services

Having the right offerings that best meets the market needs at a price that is acceptable to customers and provides profitable cash flows for the organization requires a well thoughtout product design process.

Clarifying Product Marketing Strategy

The starting point for a product marketing strategy for any business should begin with the customer. The business was built on satisfying the needs of their customers, any adjustment in marketing approaches should consider the customer as the centerpiece of the strategy, and any action taken should consider the customer's view of valuing its products.

A starting point that can be useful is to classify customers based on the amount of their spending. Spending used as a metric can help an analyst understand which customers provide the biggest impact on the business. Customer categories can be described as follows:

1. Key customers that represent high volume users,
2. Customers that have potential to provide greater sales (Under-Potential),
3. Customers that are not users (Nonusers).

This simple classification may reveal some important information. For example, a company may find that the key customers are located in a specific geography, be of a certain size, have a certain business orientation or have other characteristics that may be useful in developing marketing programs to attract new customers. This analysis may also reveal characteristics that define Nonusers of the company's products. Understanding the size of the Nonuser and Under-Potential user markets and their characteristics may also prove useful in developing marketing strategies.

The classification of customers may be enough to launch an ad campaign or promotional efforts but may not be enough to justify new product introductions or significant changes in marketing strategies.

After customers have been classified, a business can look at its various products and services and analyze them on the price versus cost to change relationship between the business and the customer. This approach measures the price charged for the product or service and compares that with the cost a customer would incur to change from the product they currently use to an alternative product offered. This may be financial cost incurred for changes in the customer's facilities or mode of operations or simply the difference in price of the products. Opportunity costs may also come into play if a customer has to forego opportunities to adopt a new product. This analysis assumes that price is the critical factor to cause a customer to change. If customer service, guarantees, maintenance, and other nonprice issues are important then additional analyses will be required.

According to this type of analysis, when there is no cost to the customer to change, there is Equilibrium. This result assumes that the customer could change to an alternative product and incur no costs associated with the change.

When the cost to the customer to change is greater than the price charged, there is a Positive Equilibrium relationship, which may provide the current product provider the ability to increase the price of the product and thereby increase the profitability without jeopardizing the relationship with the customer as long as a positive equilibrium state is maintained. Again this assumes that price is the critical factor. If other factors are important and the ability to deliver those factors to the customer difficult, then increasing the price to the customer could cause the customer to consider other vendors.

When the cost to the customer to change is less than the price charged, there is a <u>Negative Equilibrium</u> relationship, which could provide the customer a reason to find a substitute product or service. This means a customer could change products and save money. This scenario may also be an indication that the business has some special strength that is not price related. A close study of this group might be useful in setting strategies for the first two groups mentioned.

This exercise, when completed, provides a starting point for a marketing strategy because customers have been divided into smaller groups for further study. The smaller groups help analysts determine whether an action taken to affect one category of customer will have a negative impact on another customer group. For example, if a price strategy change is employed to attract more sales from Under-Potential customers who have a Positive Equilibrium status, it could result in a negative impact to Key customers in the Equilibrium or Negative Equilibrium categories.

As an example, a newspaper company might have an advertiser that would be classified as Under-Potential with Positive Equilibrium (this is a customer that still spends most of his ad dollars with other ad media and there would be a real cost to this customer to move more advertising to the newspaper).

A strategy to offer this advertiser a lower price for increases in ad expenditures that would offset his cost to move advertising to the newspaper might seem to be in order. The downside of this move might be that there are Key advertisers in the Negative Equilibrium or Equilibrium categories (these advertisers could move away from the newspaper at no cost or actually save money) who would now face competition from the newly attracted Under-Potential advertiser. This situation might result in Key customers diverting ad dollars to other media or require a price (and profit) reduction by the newspaper for Key customers in the negative equilibrium or equilibrium categories.

Another example might be a consumer who purchased groceries at a new store offering very low special pricing. As soon as this pricing reverts to the higher, nonpromotional pricing, the consumer will return to the retailer in which a positive equilibrium relationship exists.

In both of these instances, it might be better to use a marketing strategy to attract these customers that is not based on price. Product attributes other than pricing may be instrumental in marketing strategies to attract these customers.

The customer categories can be combined with the equilibrium categories so there are now three equilibrium categories for each of the customer classifications. For example, there would be Key customers that are in Equilibrium, Key customers with Positive Equilibrium, and so on.

	In Equilibrium	Positive Equilibrium	Negative Equilibrium
Key Customers			
Under-Potential Customers			
Nonusers			

Customers in Negative Equilibrium may not be concerned with price as much as much as they are with intangibles such as customer service or long-term supplier relationships. Key customers in the Negative Equilibrium category are likely to be very profitable and can be subject to special attention by competitors.

Nonusers in negative equilibrium may be those customers who belong to the competition and who purchased when their regular supplier was unable to provide product. This group could be worthy of further study and could be an opportunity to win profitable market share from the competition.

From a company point of view, the area of greatest concern would seem to be those products with a negative equilibrium relationship for their customers. Negative equilibrium means that these customers could change products and save money; thus, they are vulnerable to aggressive attack by competitors. Because this group is paying more for the product or service than they would from another source, it is very important to understand where they are placing the value of the business relationship.

It would also appear that those customers with a positive equilibrium relationship would be satisfied with the relationship with the organization because changing to another vendor would be more expensive than continuing the current business relationship. There may be an opportunity to increase pricing with this group, but it is necessary to understand how much a price can be raised before moving the customer to a category that might be likely to find another vendor. It is also important to understand whether there are other factors affecting the relationship.

Those customers in equilibrium may be worthy of in-depth analysis to determine which factors could cause them to change suppliers as price is not an issue.

Defining Potential Actions

Because price and the cost for a customer to change are the only variables measured by the above process, it may be important to include a complete description of the product and the alternatives used in the comparison. The product description should include all tangible and intangible characteristics. Tangible characteristics would include size, weight, and other physical properties of the product. Intangible characteristics would include guarantees, customer service, and ease of understanding how to use the product or product training and so on.

While tangible and intangible characteristics may be hard to capture, it is an important exercise from the view of the customer. It helps understand the real job the customer has hired the company and its products to do.

Clayton Christensen gives the example of milk shakes being used in the morning as a breakfast substitute for people on their drive to work and in the afternoon as a reward mothers gave to their children after school. In his example, the milk shake had been "hired" to do two different jobs by two different customer groups. Clearly price alone could describe neither the different jobs the product was "hired" to do nor the value of the product to either group. In the case of milk shakes, characteristics that would need to be included would be the availability of the product.[1]

To help describe product characteristics, it may be useful to consider the potential actions to be taken in light of several Consumer Adoption Drivers (CAD) that we developed at GWR Research.[2]

The Consumer Adoption Drivers are:

1. Group influence intensity—relates to peer pressure exerted on customers
2. Perishability—the length of time the product is deemed useful
3. Psychological appeal—status associated with the product
4. Price sensitivity—the need for the customer to budget for the purchase
5. Relative price influence—the attractiveness of other products as a substitute when price is a consideration
6. Frequency of purchase—the frequency with which the customer purchases the product

7. Search time intensity—the amount of time invested in the search for the "right" product
8. Tangible differentiability—physical differences between products
9. Intangible differentiability—nonphysical differences between products (guarantees, relationships with company, branding, etc.)
10. Technical complexity—the need for training before a customer can use the product. This may be a factor in determining the type of sales force that will be required.

The following table arranges each dimension next to a semantic differential. Using a fairly simple research survey, customers can rank the dimensions as being of high, low, or no importance. Analysts can use questions that elicit responses for each CAD descriptor.

Dimension	High	Low	None
Group influence intensity			
Perishability			
Psychological appeal			
Price sensitivity			
Relative price influence			
Frequency of purchase			
Search time intensity			
Tangible differentiability			
Intangible differentiability			
Technical complexity			

Customer Survey Process

Using focus groups to get a qualitative feel may provide a good start to identifying customer groups according to CAD.

For critical strategic decisions, customer groups surveyed should be large enough to provide results with a high level of statistical confidence. The key customer and underpotential customer categories may require a census to provide statistically significant findings. Nonuser categories are likely large enough to use random-sampling techniques.

To make the analysis easier, the questionnaires would note which of the nine categories (Equilibrium Key customers, Positive Equilibrium

Key customers, and so on) the customer belonged. This allows responses to be collected and analyzed by customer type.

Analysis of the Data

Using luxury automobile consumers, an example of the CAD analysis is shown as follows:

The following symbols are used to show how each equilibrium category responded:

+ Represents Positive Equilibrium customers

– Represents Negative Equilibrium customers

= Represents customers in Equilibrium

Key Customers—Luxury Automobile Consumers

	GII	Perish	Psy. a	Price	RPI	FOP	STI	TD	ID	TC
High	+		+			+	–	+	+	
		–					=	–	–	
		=					+	=		
Low	–	+		+	+	–				–
		–		–	–	=				+
		=								=
None	=			=	=				=	

Under-Potential Customers—Luxury Automobile Consumers

	GII	Perish	Psy. a	Price	RPI	FOP	STI	TD	ID	TC
High		+	+	+	+		+	+	–	
		–	–				=	–		
		=	=					*		
Low	+			=	=	–			=	–
	–					+	–		+	+
	=					=				=
None				·	·					

For the Key customer categories of this company with positive equilibrium (they would need to spend more money than they are now to adopt the luxury automobile), Group Influence Intensity was considered high.

This means that the action of their peers would influence the type of luxury car they would purchase.

For those key customers that had negative equilibrium (they could change and save money), Group Influence Intensity was low. Group Influence Intensity did not affect key customers that were in equilibrium. One could conclude then that certain key customers are influenced by their peers to purchase a particular luxury automobile while others were not. One could then assume that a marketing strategy that used individuals viewed as peers in ads would have a positive effect on the positive equilibrium consumers and no effect on the negative equilibrium or equilibrium consumers (a seemingly safe strategy).

For Under-Potential customers, it might be useful to target consumers in the negative equilibrium category as price is of little consideration to this group. What is important is intangible differentiability. A marketing campaign focusing on the brand might be beneficial here and would not have a negative effect on any of the other key customer categories. Combining use of peer groups and brand in an ad might have the effect of reaching the key customer and Under-Potential customer categories effectively.

The process of using the CAD and cross-referencing the customer categories can be used as idea generators for strategic marketing initiatives. These initiatives can then be measured against a set of criteria that helps analysts and managers focus on overall organizational goals.

A Navigational Tool to Identify the Best Actions

Listed below is a set of criteria that we have successfully used for new product development and strategic planning. These criteria helped planners ensure that actions that moved on to the implementation stage were consistent with the organization's overall goals.

1. Profit—Does this action improve the profitability of the organization? If not, is there a compelling reason for this action other than profit?
2. Credibility—Does this action enhance the organization's position with its core customer segments? Is it closely related to the kind of business we are in?

3. Image—Does this action enhance the organization's image? For example, if we are upscale, does the action enhance this image?
4. Resources—What resources are required? What is the internal rate of return?
5. Gateway Capacity—Does this action have the capacity to broaden market opportunities for the organization?
6. Negative Gateway Capacity—Does this strategy have the capacity to expose the organization to negative publicity or potential litigation?

Implementation of Chosen Actions

Success for this process depends on continual involvement by executives from each discipline in the organization's leadership. There should be a team formed of these executives that meets regularly (weekly) during the strategic review process.

The executive review team should have a representative from sales, finance, operations, marketing, human resources etc. Representation of the different business disciplines assures that internal perspectives are considered for all potential actions.

An individual should be chosen from the group that will act as its leader and keep the team focused on producing results. Meetings should be held separately from other business meetings and functions to underscore the importance of the exercise.

The review process will likely take several weeks to several months to complete depending on the level of analysis desired at each step of the review process.

The Caller-Times Market Assessment

The approach described above was first used at the *Corpus Christi Caller-Times*. The general manager wanted some direction on how to address the changes taking place that affected newspaper advertising.

Market changes included:

1. A few newspapers had introduced zoned supplements to attract one-location advertisers that served only part of the market.

2. A new direct mail entrant, ADVO, had discovered how to combine several advertisers' circulars into one package so mail costs could be shared. This new approach appeared to be a threat to circulars being delivered as part of the newspaper.
3. There were new free publications that contained "want ads" that competed directly with the newspaper's classified sections.

We initiated a full market study and the process took about 6 months and involved all of the key department executives.

The study found that:

1. There were Key advertisers who might use alternative advertising delivery products if introduced, particularly in areas of low circulation penetration,
2. There were small advertisers who wanted to advertise in the *Caller-Times* but could not afford the cost of an ad and did not need the benefit of the newspaper's full circulation,
3. There was a high concentration of Nonuser and Under-Potential advertisers in two geographic areas,
4. There was a concentration of Nonuser and Under-Potential advertisers in the service and financial business sectors.
5. An opportunity existed to introduce niche publications to advertisers needing to target certain audiences (ethnic, entertainment etc.),
6. An opportunity existed to offer advertisers direct mail capabilities.

After studying the findings, the group of executives generated a list of potential alternative actions based on a CAD analysis. After deliberation and debate, a total of 15 programs were listed as potential strategic marketing initiatives.

These programs included:

1. "Zoning" of the daily newspaper, which allowed news and advertising to be delivered by geographic areas,
2. "Zoning" a section of the newspaper and overthrowing the section to households that did not subscribe to the newspaper,

3. Establishing a separate product to be delivered to nonsubscribers only,
4. Restructuring the sales organization by customer type,
5. Development of an alternative carrier delivery program for delivery of ad circulars,
6. Development of a direct mail program for advertisers,
7. Revamping the classified section of the newspaper,
8. Reducing rates for advertisers with small businesses,
9. Establishing several niche products.

After considerable study of the potential program and using the customer segmentation and the navigational tools described above, the task group decided to consider:

1. Launching a "zoned" section of the newspaper that would be included as a section of newspaper subscribers' newspapers and delivered to nonsubscribers for free,
2. Launching a newspaper section delivered by alternative carrier force to nonsubscribers only,
3. Launching a direct mail program,
4. Launching a "zoned" delivery program to deliver advertising circulars in the newspaper to specific geographic areas,
5. Launching a classified-only product for autos and other vehicles that would be available free at various retail outlets,
6. Restructuring the ad sales staff.

Each of these programs then went into a product evaluation phase to determine whether they were economically viable and would be accepted by the marketplace. This phase involved a concept test where mock-ups were presented to groups of advertisers to determine whether they would advertise the products, and if so how much and how often they would advertise.

The concept testing showed that

1. A "zoned" section of the newspaper that was also delivered to non-subscribers,
2. A direct mail program,

3. An auto-classified product,

4. A zoned ad circular program, and

5. A modified restructuring of the sales force would be in order.

Interestingly, a price reduction for advertising was not needed.

This process was also introduced at the *Houston Chronicle* and *San Francisco Chronicle* and resulted in the launch of direct mail programs, specialty publications, utilization of broker sales organizations, and niche products.

Review of the Rationale Behind a Market Assessment

The purpose of establishing segments, prioritizing the segments in order of those needing attention and analyzing the prioritized segments against the CAD is to make certain that strategy is considered from the customer's point of view. The use of criteria to measure the appropriateness of the considered strategic moves helps managers keep initiatives within the bounds of an organization's overarching goals.

This process helps identify what should be done to counteract disruptions that are impacting the market due to general innovation or environment change and what can be done to correct or improve things that are within the business management's control. It helps identify those actions that are price-related and that will affect profit and further stresses options that are available that may be used in lieu of price-related actions.

Any size organization can implement all or part of this process. The process instills a disciplined approach of addressing strategic marketing issues and helps improve an organization's chance of choosing the optimal marketing options.

New Product Development

As markets and customer preferences change, companies adapt to ensure success. Adaptations usually are made to capitalize on markets and expertise a firm has developed over its life.

Some adaptations are limited to updating packaging or marketing approaches or finding new uses for established products.

There are occasions where new products are needed to meet new customer needs or address a disruptive market innovation.

When addressing changing market needs and market disruptions, it is necessary to find good ideas and then have a process to evaluate and narrow the field to the ideas most likely to succeed.

Generating New Product Ideas

The first step in generating good ideas that will further develop the markets and expertise that defines the firm is to clearly articulate the job customers are hiring the firm to perform. This should be in line with the original mission and vision statement.

Here it is important not to be too restrictive in the focus of the definition. It is probably better for an owner of a baseball team to define his firm's job as sports entertainment as opposed to the more focused definition of professional baseball.

As most newspaper owners are aware, it is better for them to be in the business of providing information rather than strictly the newspaper business. This allows newspaper publishers to consider multiple platforms to deliver information.

Once the job the customer has hired the company to perform is defined, it will be easier to identify new product ideas that are based on the firm's strengths.

There are several methods to develop new product ideas that are very useful such as brainstorming, market research, and product attribute modeling.

Brainstorming is widely used and involves getting key employees (and sometimes customers) together to find solutions to challenges facing the firm. The key to successful brainstorming is good note taking, allowing all ideas to be presented without negative feedback, and encouraging all participants to contribute without letting a few dominate the exercise.

Market research can be the result of research surveys designed to uncover market opportunities. This research involves current customers, individuals with characteristics similar to current customers, or a random selection of individuals. Examining a firm's records and reviewing sales staff information on the market and the competition can also provide solid market research. Focus groups are an inexpensive way to define customer's needs and test new product ideas.

Product attribute modeling is a unique way of generating new product ideas by choosing a job the company is hired to perform and describing the absolute worst outcomes. After identifying the bad outcomes, participants go back through the exercise and determine what actions could be taken to eliminate the negative outcomes. For example, if a company made suitcases, an exercise might be to list all of the negative attributes for suitcases (such as not fitting in overhead bins in aircraft, wheels that wobbled, instability, etc.). The follow-up exercise would be to create a suitcase that addressed all of the negative attributes.

The best idea generation will likely come from a program that involves all of the idea-generation techniques: first, market research, then brainstorming based on the research, and finally product attribute modeling.

Identifying the Best Ideas

After the idea generation process, there are likely to be a number of ideas that are attractive. The challenge is to find a way of objectively identifying those ideas that have the most promise.

For this process it is important to assemble a committee of key employees from each part of the business. The committee should have members from sales, IT, finance, accounting, production, R&D, and engineering. This structure allows any idea to have the insights of the various parts of the organization. The committee should be led by an individual who can keep the group generating customer-focused ideas and prevent efforts to kill product ideas because they do not fit with current thinking.

When evaluating new product ideas, just as when marketing strategy is being evaluated, there should be specific criteria identified that the new product must meet before moving to the next level of consideration. A list of evaluation criteria, similar to that used in the previous section, might look like the following:

1. Profitability/market acceptability—will the product generate a profit and a market?
2. Accreditation requirements—Does the product meet industry and legal standards?

3. Length of project—Can the product be introduced in an acceptable time frame?

4. Accommodate systems—Does the new product make use of current systems or will new ones need to be developed?

5. Fit image—Does the product fit the image the firm wishes to project?

6. Resources—Is the new product resource and capital intensive?

7. Gateway capacity—Does this product lead to the possibility of new products or businesses being developed?

8. Negative gateway capacity—Does this product have the potential of damaging other aspects of the operation?

9. Customer acceptance—Will the customer accept this product over others offered in the market?

If product ideas successfully meet all of the criteria, then product ideas can be chosen to move forward to a product planning process. Those chosen as having the highest priority should best meet all of the criteria with the least organizational expense.

Product Planning

Product planning requires that the participants of the committee review each product based on its impact on their area of operations. This review should include all phases of the organization from design to production, marketing, and billing. This review will bring to light areas of concern that will need to be addressed before final planning begins.

The final plans that this committee produces will include financial proformas and projections, marketing plans and goals, operational plans and identification points or outcomes that would result in termination or reevaluation of the project.

In the end, executive management will approve or disapprove the project, but they will feel certain that the new products presented have had the benefit of a rigorous, objective process to create products that are most likely to have a positive outcome for the company.

At the *Corpus Christi Caller-Times*, we developed this process for reviewing our customers and the markets we served to create new products and revenue streams. This program was so successful I used it at every opportunity. In Houston, we created a new product committee and enjoyed all the successes and breakthroughs I had come to expect from cross-functional teams.

Over the years, I was able to attend new product seminars and meet with the leaders of companies that had sophisticated new product development processes. I met with new product managers from Ford, 3M, Proctor and Gamble, and others. It was clear that teams were a critical element of new product development but so was a process. In every case, these leading new product developers had a series of steps that took new products from the idea stage to the market. Most companies used a stage-gate process, which reviewed the product at each stage of development. If the product met pre-established expectations, then the product was allowed to move to the next stage of development.

We created a similar process at the *Houston Chronicle*, which was then adopted by the *Hearst* newspaper group. We found that we were able to have several ideas and projects under review simultaneously and move good ideas into good products at a very fast pace (See Exhibit 7-1).

Ideas were accepted from anyone. Employees and customers provided the most actionable ideas. The first step was to evaluate the project in a broad sense. Did it compliment the other businesses we operated and

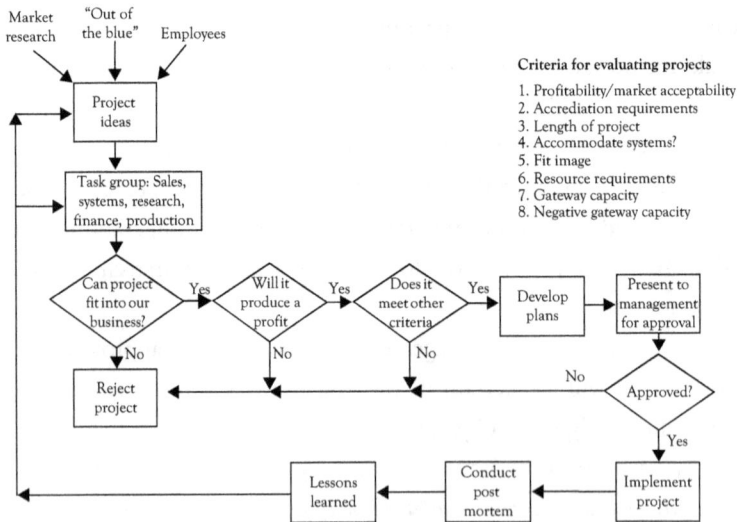

Exhibit 7-1. New Product Development Process.[3] Copyright GWR Research

customers we served? Could it produce a profit? We chose only projects serving our markets and that would produce at least a 30% operating margin.

The next step was to screen projects based on their ability to create new revenue streams. This would require that they would create a market demand, be easy for our sales force to present to new and established customers and fit well with our product mix and our operating systems.

We also considered the product's "gateway capacity" or its ability to generate additional products. For example, one of the reasons we chose to develop a relationship with the Spanish language publication "*La Voz*" was its ability to provide access to the Hispanic market and ultimately produce an array of products for that market.

The *La Voz* project not only filled the goal of reaching the Hispanic market but also taught us how to work with niche print publishers. Over the next few years, the *Chronicle* entered into printing and distribution relationships with several niche publishers.

CHAPTER 8

Promotion

Moving an Audience to Act

Starting with the Consumer Adoption Drivers (CAD) discussed in the previous chapter should provide some direction in developing communications to targeted customer segments. For instance, in the luxury automobile example, it appeared that group influence was important to key customers in positive equilibrium and of low importance to customers in negative equilibrium. It also appeared that both groups found that tangible differentiability was of high importance. One potential communication strategy then might be to create ads that focused on the physical attributes of the car. This would avoid any potential conflict from using individuals in the ads portraying roles of peers to the targeted audience.

Once the advertising approach is determined, the strategy of media and use comes into play.

Because advertising is the primary method for businesses to inform and influence individuals to consider and purchase their products, the question is often asked, "How many advertising exposures are needed to cause an individual to act?" Unfortunately, there is no formula available to answer this question but there are considerations that can help.

Roger Wimmer points out that *all* people must pass through five stages to make a decision about anything or learn anything. These stages are (1) Unawareness, (2) Awareness, (3) Comprehension, (4) Conviction, and (5) Action.

If bringing an audience from the stage of Unawareness to the final stage of Action is the goal, the frequency of exposure to an advertising message will be much higher than that which is required for just moving the audience from Conviction to Action.

Moving through all five stages probably would involve a product or concept that is new to the audience and the initial communications would have to educate the audience. The more complicated the product or concept, the greater the education requirements will be. For example, introducing a new drink to a market familiar with drink products will require less education than introducing insurance to an audience unfamiliar with the concept.

Moving from conviction to action is seemingly the easiest and should require the least number of messages to result in favorable action. This however is not necessarily the case. An individual may know there is a need for a product but may be hesitant to make a purchase due to budgetary restraints or the inability to make a choice from many similar products.

Identifying the Audience

Most businesses have a good idea of the composition of the target audience to receive advertising messages. The managers know the products, their uses, and the intended audiences. The audience demographic profiles can be fairly broad to very specific. For example, introducing a new computer would suggest those individuals who use a computer are the targeted audience of an ad message for the computer introduction. Since computer users come in every sex, age, or other demographic profile the ad campaign should have a broad audience reach.

Offering new roofing can be more specifically targeted to individuals who own homes 25 years old or older who have not purchased a new roof.

Classifying customers using the CAD techniques identified in the *Clarifying Marketing Strategy* section of the previous chapter can be very helpful here.

Before designing an ad or message, it is recommended that some time be spent on understanding the audience by identifying the stage of the persuasion cycle, the demographic profile, and the specific message to deliver. In some cases, a general message delivered through a general reach media provides an efficient, effective means of moving individuals to action. In other instances, a specifically directed message to an individual may be needed to result in action.

Understanding Media and Its Value to the Audience

Choosing the right media for an advertising message should be considered as important as understanding the audience. Broad reach media should be considered effective when:

1. The audience is broad such as computer users or homeowners,
2. The product or concept is new and requires audience education,
3. The product is well known and is available from many sources, or
4. The product has different uses by different audiences.

More targeted media should be considered effective when:

1. The audience can be identified by 3 or more demographic characteristics,
2. The audience has a specific interest,
3. The audience has a specific ethnic, age, industry, or target profile, or if,
4. Individuals or small clusters of individuals are targeted.

General circulation newspapers are an effective media for broad market reach. In 2012, 42.9 % of total adults in the United States read a newspaper daily and 44.0% read a newspaper on Sunday.[1] Advertising messages can be placed in various sections of the newspaper to reach certain subjects such as sports and entertainment audiences. Newspapers also allow preprinted inserts that can be "zoned" to be distributed in specific zip codes or geographic areas.

Direct mail and shared mail programs provide the ability to reach the broader market or very targeted markets. The U.S. Postal Service reports that 74% of households read direct mail advertising weekly. Ad messages can be tailored to specific individuals or can be a uniform message to all recipients.

Radio and television have a broad reach but generally cannot duplicate the reach demonstrated by newspapers or direct mail. Radio and television lend themselves to distributing messages to demographically unique groups that watch or listen to certain programming. While the viewing or listening audience may be large and diverse, radio and TV audiences usually will be smaller than those reached by a general circulation newspaper or a full market mailing.

Ethnic media provide the ability to reach meaningful audiences in a large diverse market. For example in Houston, Texas, there are newspapers for the African American, Hispanic, Jewish, Chinese, Pakistani, and East Indian communities. Advertising in ethnic media may open access to markets that are not available through traditional media. These communities are large enough to represent significant purchasing power for products offered, and the publications are usually reasonably priced.

The Internet has the ability to reach general and targeted audiences. An ad placed for general viewing on a high traffic site such as Google will be exposed to a wide array of web surfers. An ad that employs key word searches can direct a very targeted audience to an ad or Web site.

Targeted or niche publications reach audiences that are smaller and have more defined characteristics but may still be quite general in nature. A Vietnamese newspaper in a large metropolitan area would still reach individuals who have a wide array of needs and interests. Trade magazines would reach more defined professional groups that comprise a large number of demographic profiles.

Outdoor advertising has the ability to reach the general audiences or targeted groups through the number and geographic placement of signage.

If an audience is reached by a media, it does not mean the advertising message will be received. The ad may not be welcomed in certain media. The term "junk mail" was coined as a phrase describing advertising mail that cluttered the recipient's mailbox. TIVo and cable ready program recording systems allow television viewers to eliminate advertising messages. The popularity of these programs suggests that in certain instances advertising is not welcomed. On the Internet, the ability to screen "junk" email and close or prevent "pop-up" advertising also suggests that ad messages are not wanted at times.

What Is Effective Frequency?

Effective frequency is the number of times a message needs to be delivered to the right audience to result in action and is within the cost constraints of the advertising budget. Effective frequency requires that the advertiser understand the audience, the stage of the persuasion process, the cost of delivering the message, and the best media to deliver the message.

For most products, the general audience media is the best place to start unless the intended audience is a very small subset of the general population. General audience advertising can be supported with more targeted media to promote action. For example, adding ethnic publications may be a good way to reinforce advertising in the broader reach newspaper. These messages followed up with messages through the Internet key word searches or direct mailing will further enhance the ability to move audiences to action.

Another approach is to support a series of ads in a targeted media with fewer ads in a general audience media. Directing messages through key word searches, direct mail, or targeted publications for specific audiences can be enhanced by an overarching ad in a general market media outlet.

The frequency of ads will generally be determined by an advertising budget. The mix of ad media should maximize the number of messages delivered to the targeted audience. If the budget is very limited and the target market is small, a well thought-out series of direct mail or email messages may be appropriate. For example, a direct mailing to 10,000 CEOs might cost between $5,000 and $10,000. If there were 10 messages needed to educate the CEO audience and lead them to action, a $100,000 budget would be required. An email campaign could cost less.

If the desired audience were all CEOs in a large area, a general circulation newspaper would be a good choice. For around $10,000, a quarter page ad can be purchased in most major newspapers. If 10 messages were required, the newspaper budget would be $100,000. A positive consequence of this form of advertising is the reach of non-CEOs who would also have interest in the product. If the total number of CEOs in the market were 150,000, a direct mailing follow-up might be prohibitive and could be replaced with an email or niche product advertising campaign.

Why Aren't They Buying My Products?

Understanding the relationship of customer needs, customer adoption inertia, and the content of the marketing message are critical.

Mary Kay once answered the above question with "I didn't ask them to buy". Clearly, asking the customer to purchase is key to closing the sale but a lot has to go into producing a sale before you get to that point.

There's much to be said about a product's offerings and the reputation of the company producing the product. But in the final analysis, it is a combination of the product fitting with the customer's needs, the ease with which the customer can change from current products, and the ease to explain product benefits to the customer that result in success.

Furthermore, it is not just one of these attributes but all three in concert that make the difference between a product failure and a smashing success.

Understanding the Customers' Needs

When considering the customer, it's always a good idea to try to walk in their shoes. Or rather, if you were a customer, why would you change products?

We started a daily newspaper in Huntsville, Texas, the *Huntsville Morning News*. The local business leaders promised their support and pledged $2 million in financial support. What followed was an extraordinary project that built a newspaper plant, acquired initial subscribers, created editorial, production, delivery, and financial and marketing capabilities and published its first newspaper all within 90 days. This feat caught the competition flat-footed and allowed the *Morning News* to win market share.

A couple of months after opening the doors, we were not happy with the revenue we were receiving from local businesses that had invested in our newspaper. Indeed, the preponderance of their ad expenditure was still in the other newspaper. I asked one of the key businessmen why this was so and his response was telling. He said, "I have to make sure my business succeeds."

While he was willing to make a financial investment in a new venture, he did not believe the new newspaper would replace the results produced by the established newspaper. Rather, he thought it might bring in supplemental customers who might be new readers.

Unfortunately, this was the view of most of the business leaders and just as unfortunate the *Huntsville Morning News* success was dependent on winning the lion's share of the local businesses ad budgets.

This newspaper battle lasted about a year before we ran out of money and had not built a cash flow that would support the business. While there is evidence there could have been a successful outcome, the reality was we did not create a business that could beat the competition and survive.

We did not understand that our primary customers' needs were growing their businesses. We did not focus on this outcome and adjust the strategy to being a secondary ad buy for these business leaders. We did not adjust the strategy to accommodate a longer lead-time to go from a supplemental advertising vehicle to the primary ad buy. We did not change our message to ask for a portion of the ad budget at the outset and then demonstrate the benefit of moving more ad spending to our newspaper over time and the final result was a failed business.

Later when at the *Houston Chronicle*, we were given the challenge of creating a direct mail product. At the time, the leading distributor for weekly grocery circulars along with other retailers was a marriage mail product delivered by ADVO. ADVO had built its business on a concept of sharing mail costs by getting advertisers to put their sales circulars together in one mail package and sharing the mail costs. The result for advertisers was a lower cost for the same ad exposure.

When we were given this challenge, Houston was ADVO's most profitable market and the *Houston Chronicle* had a small part of advertising budgets from advertisers using ADVO's products.

We knew that advertising in the *Houston Chronicle* was better read than direct mail. In fact, direct mail had earned the moniker of "junk mail" because some recipients just tossed the mailed ads in the trash. The problem we faced was that the *Chronicle* was subscribed to by roughly half of the community's households whereas mail was delivered to every household. Reaching all households was a critical feature for ADVO and its customers.

After some study we determined that we could combine delivery of the newspaper to subscribers with mail delivery for nonsubscribers at a lower cost than shared mail and with roughly half going to newspaper *Chronicle* subscriber homes that had a better readership of advertising.

Thus, we could deliver the same number of households as ADVO with better results at a lower cost. This met the test of matching the customers' needs but hurdles remained.

Understanding Customer Adoption Inertia

If the adoption process requires a significant change in a customer's routine or requires an education process, then customers might not buy. This was true with the *Chronicle*'s ad delivery program.

To move advertisers from a product where they knew the results to a product where results were unknown created a risk to the business that had to be overcome. To accomplish this, we broke the adoption process down to digestible chunks of business that could be moved to the *Chronicle* to test the outcome. Fortunately, the test outcome was favorable and over the next year or so, most of the business that had used marriage mail products in Houston shifted to the *Chronicle*'s program.

Another of the interesting challenges with the *Houston Chronicle*'s mail program was the pricing. Subscriber penetration was not identical in every zip code and so delivery costs would vary by zip code. One approach to this would have required that advertisers pick and choose zip codes based on cost. This might have had some advantages but would have created such a change from how advertisers placed ad orders that adoption of the program would have suffered. We really had to study our pricing structure to make sure we produced a profit and still allowed the advertiser maximum flexibility and ease of use. In the end, advertisers were able to adopt a superior product with no change in how they operated their business. This became a critical component of the marketing and promotion communications to our advertisers.

Understanding What the Message Should Be

If you have developed a superior product that meets the customers' needs and made it easy to adopt, you may still find that your marketing message can be the problem.

When I helped found a new commercial real estate sales company, American Property Data (APD), in Houston, Texas, the concept was unique in that our company would attract listings from commercial brokers all over the country and present those listings to qualified investment groups located all over the country.

Success depended on attracting a leading commercial real estate broker in each market willing to sign on as an affiliate and feed their listings into the system.

Success also depended on qualified investors subscribing to our services and ultimately purchasing properties through our system.

Getting investors to subscribe to the service was relatively simple. If you were a qualified investor, a small subscription fee would certainly be a worthwhile investment.

Brokers, on the other hand, had to agree to a significant fee to be the exclusive affiliate in a market and had to be willing to share commissions on any property sold through the system.

There was no question that APD was built around the needs of a commercial broker by providing a means of exposing his properties to groups of qualified buyers. This would not only allow the broker to increase sales but also to attract more listings and attract the best commercial real estate agents to work with the broker.

In addition, the broker would not have to change how they operated their business. They would simply have a new tool that promised more sales opportunities.

The marketing communication difficulty encountered in the beginning was centered on our infatuation with the system's sophistication. In the beginning, we talked about how the database was able to identify needs according to buyers' specifications and how we were able to have computers in buyers' and brokers' offices updated daily with new property information.

Unfortunately, it was not the sophistication of the system that brokers were interested in. That information could come later. Eventually we learned the marketing message had to describe the benefits in terms that most mattered to brokers—getting more and better listings and attracting the best real estate agents.

This lesson was not lost when it came time to introduce the *Houston Chronicle*'s delivery system. Our program was presented by *Chronicle*'s senior staff members to advertising buying decision makers. The message was simple—the *Chronicle* can reach all of the households currently being reached for a lower cost and better results.

It would be later that we would talk about the sophistication of databases and the ability to customize delivery. Interestingly, it was the customized delivery that allowed us to expand advertising delivery and commercial printing and produce new streams of profitable revenue.

Fitting Them Together

Successful product introductions require financial, logistics, and personnel expertise, but all of this may be a waste if the customer is not the absolute focus of the overall process. Managers and engineers have to put their egos in the backseat and take the customer's view. Marketing messages have to emphasize how products address the customer's needs and the ease of adopting the product.

When we first began working on the *Houston Chronicle*'s mail program, we were committed to using the *Chronicle*'s carrier delivery to nonsubscribers instead of the mail. We had good reasons to want to use the *Chronicle*'s system. It had lower operating costs, it would give more reasons for readers to use our carrier-delivered nonsubscriber products, and it would give us ultimate control of product development. This reasoning was clearly not customer-centric.

After several meetings with key managers and the feedback from customers, we determined that we would have to use mail to be successful. It did not matter how good our rationalizations were if they were not focused solely on the customer.

Being customer-centric followed through to allowing advertisers to adopt the program in nonthreatening, digestible portions and gearing our communications to showing how our system matched the customers' needs. In the end, the *Chronicle*'s new ad delivery system became the market leader and remains so today.

Using the CAD process can help determine the marketing strategy and choose the appropriate media. Continued focus on the customer will help design the marketing messages in a way that underscores meeting the needs identified by CAD and reassuring the customer that product adoption will be easy and beneficial.

CHAPTER 9

Pricing

The impact of pricing strategies can be critical for the success of new product launches, a company's image and ultimately a company's short- and long-term success.

When, according to a Consumer Adoption Drivers analysis, the price sensitivity factor is high, individuals are willing to spend more time searching for the "right" price. These purchases usually relate to the amount of the individual's budget being spent for the product or service. So for the "right" price, customers are willing to travel farther and less affected by other product attributes. The "right" price is not necessarily the lowest price, rather, it is the price most willingly paid when all of the product attributes are considered.

Reacting to the Competition

Basing price on a competitor's pricing approach is fraught with hazards.

I have worked in several industries and found that pricing is often overlooked as a key marketing tool. In many instances, pricing is driven by the sales department and is a reaction to the competition. This reaction assumes the competition knows the market better and has a superior marketing strategy.

When reacting to the competition, it is important to understand that you are being drawn into a game whereby you play by the competitor's rules. You are playing their game and changing your strategy. Your hope here is that you can play the game better or that the competitors cannot play their own game very well.

I am reminded of a time where my company was vying for the business of a key customer. The customer was a shrewd negotiator. We understood the value of the customer but valued profit and the perception that our product commanded a higher price. The customer, we knew, would use the price bids to play the competitors against each other.

Our belief was that this was a no-win strategy and decided to bid the price to the point where we would make very little profit and then let the competitor win the bid. We felt that winning the bid was the end game for our competitor, and we took the risk that they would lower the price until they won the contract.

Fortunately, we were right, competition won the contract but could not provide the needed level of service. The customer ultimately canceled the contract with the competitor and chose to pay our price for our product. As a result, we were able to service the account and make a profit.

If we had chosen to win the contract, thereby adopting the competitor's strategy, we would have lost money, possibly hurt relations with our good customers who were willing to pay a reasonable price for a good product and earned a reputation as a company that placed short-term market share gain over long-term success.

Pricing to Increase Volume

Lowering price to increase sales volumes can have an adverse affect on the overall marketing strategy.

Pricing can be driven by financial need and the belief that dropping prices will increase sales volume and profitability. This approach is based on the belief that the product has positive price elasticity. Positive price elasticity holds that as prices drop, demand increases enough to ensure that the lower margin per unit sold is offset by increased sales volume to the extent that overall profit actually increases.

Using reductions in price to increase volume usually works for a commoditized product that has wide use. This approach usually fails if the product is designed for a specialized use or if the marketing strategy is designed to differentiate the product from others in the marketplace. For differentiated products, the volumes and profits might increase with a price reduction but the value of the efforts to differentiate the product is lost.

Pricing at the Conroe Morning News

As I mentioned in an earlier chapter, I was recruited to take the helm of a company that was in a losing battle for a market that was judged to be large enough to support only one company. The company that I led (The *Conroe Morning News*) was weaker, had limited financial reserves, and was losing money. This company's pricing strategy had been adopted to reduce price to gain volume and market share.

After studying the sales volume, I found that regardless of the past-pricing strategies, the sales volume had remained constant. To me, this meant that there was a specific value that was provided that was wanted and needed by the consumers. Based on this information, I implemented a 17% rate increase. The action terrified the sales group, and the owner's feared financial disaster. Fortunately, sales volumes remained constant, and the company went from a loss to a profit in 6 weeks.

In this instance, it would have been easy to assume the company's products did not have specific value and that the only way to increase profitability was to keep prices low and slash expenses. We, of course, also reduced expenses dramatically, but the expense reductions alone would not have saved the company. If we had kept the pricing low, we would have failed as an enterprise and sent the message to our customers and our sales staff that our products were no different from others in the marketplace and had no intrinsic value.

Pricing Based on Direct Costs

Marking up a product based on its direct cost may not recognize the value of the product when compared with other market alternatives.

Pricing can be based on the information provided by cost accounting that if variable or direct costs are covered, profits can be made. This is indeed valuable information but pricing based on direct costs only concerns itself with the costs of direct materials and labor to produce the product. This strategy is often used when adding a new product to the product mix and is influenced by the need to give the new product every opportunity to succeed.

It also heroically assumes that the established product mix covers fixed costs. This assumption does not account for subtle increases that are difficult to measure such as repair and maintenance costs and administrative costs, which are usually considered as fixed.

Pricing a New Product

At one point, I was chairing a new products committee that had developed a new product that had a great deal of promise. The competing products in the market used different production processes, and the pricing was significantly higher than was needed to cover our direct costs.

There were several on the committee that suggested that our pricing be just above our direct costs, which would, theoretically, allow us to quickly capture the market.

It is important to recognize that customers do not adopt new products based on price, particularly, if they are satisfied with the results they receive from the products they currently purchase. I argued that a significantly lower price would not recognize the organizational expense and overhead costs and could possibly suggest to our customers that our product was not equal to the competition because price is often associated with value.

We chose the higher pricing strategy because we felt our product was superior to that of the competition. It took several years to fully penetrate the market, but eventually we did capture the market and enjoyed significant sales and profit levels.

If we had adopted the direct-cost pricing model we would have been unable to afford the customer training and interface that was required to have a successful product launch. We also would have been unable to weather the time it took to penetrate the market. The customer training and interface costs were not apparent in the planning phase of the new product and were not considered in the direct-cost model.

Without adoption by the customers, the product would have been labeled a loser and dropped from the product offerings. If the direct-cost model had been used and the quality reduced to allow for customer training costs, the customer adoption would have been more problematic because there would have been less differentiation from the product already in use by customers.

Because the pricing strategy was based on value, the product never showed a loss using fully allocated costing models, and, in the end, this product captured the market and for years has been a major source of revenue and profit streams.

Using Industry Norms for Pricing

Understanding industry-pricing norms is critical when entering a new line of business.

Houston Chronicle *Commercial Printing Pricing*

The *Houston Chronicle* bought a commercial printing plant and routinely sold printing to their advertisers. The printing was primarily circulars that were inserted into newspapers. The *Chronicle* focused on selling large production runs to large advertisers.

Newspapers typically charge advertisers for space and color when they place an ad in the newspaper. Creating the ad and production work prior to publishing the ad is generally considered part of the cost of the ad, and advertisers do not receive an extra charge for this work.

Commercial printers, however, routinely charge for any work preparing a piece for printing. They charge for artwork, color separations, and prepress work.

The *Chronicle* had moved into the commercial printing arena but had failed to adopt the commercial printing revenue model. As a result, the *Chronicle*'s commercial printing was not very profitable.

When I joined the *Chronicle*, I was reviewing financial records on a major advertiser's commercial printing work and found that there were no charges for any color or production work. I then met with the customer and said that we would begin charging for these services. The customer was aware of commercial printing costs and accepted the new charges without hesitation.

The lesson here is that when a firm decides to create a new revenue stream, it is a good idea to understand how the revenue streams are created to make certain that money is not left on the table.

Pricing to Increase Revenue Streams

It is important to understand how manufacturing capabilities can provide multiple-pricing strategies.

Houston Chronicle ChronDirect *Pricing Strategy*

The *ChonDirect* program created at the *Houston Chronicle* that combined newspaper delivery with mail delivery of ad circulars required a detailed understanding of how mail costs varied with the type of delivery. To be competitive with other marriage mail programs, the *Chronicle* had to make use of the same postal rates and earn the same discounts.

Marriage mail programs used saturation mail meaning that the mail packages went to all households on a mail delivery route. The *Chronicle* would be mailing only to households that did not receive the newspaper.

Because marriage mail went to every household, the mail packages were not addressed but accompanied by a card with the address. This allowed the mail carrier to have a stack of ad packages that could be placed in any mailbox because all households received the same package. This also meant that under that mail program, the marriage mail programs could not customize ad packages for delivery to different households.

We found that by addressing the mail in carrier delivery sequence, we could match the postal discounts given to the competition, and it was required that we have every address, newspaper subscriber, and non-newspaper subscriber in carrier delivery sequence in our database. While this was a bit more cumbersome, it allowed us to cross-reference various databases with household addresses and provide customized mail packages for advertisers. For example, we were able to cross-reference home ownership and provide a roofing company with addresses of homeowners who had held the same address for 10 or more years.

The *Chronicle* had mail-packaging machinery that could be programmed to assemble marriage mail and newspaper circular packages by address. That is, each address could have a different set of ads based on demographics. The piece mail cost of delivering these packages would be the same as for marriage mail companies delivering a noncustomized saturation mail product to each address.

For pricing purposes, it provided an opportunity for the *Chronicle* to provide normal saturation rates for delivering undifferentiated packages and to charge a premium for custom packages.

The customized product became so popular that at one point a grocer was delivering 96 different versions of their weekly circular to different neighborhoods in Houston.

Pricing to Eliminate Confusion

Eliminating confusing aspects of product pricing can improve market acceptance.

The Houston Chronicle ThisWeek *Pricing Strategy*

The *Houston Chronicle* created a series of local community newspapers (*ThisWeek*) to serve the different city and suburban neighborhoods. The pricing for these products compared when competing with neighborhood newspapers. Usually these newspapers based their pricing on the number of copies delivered in the community because the newspapers were delivered free to every residence.

The *Chronicle* delivered its product to all residences as well. Subscribers received the community newspaper as a section of the *Chronicle*, and the nonsubscribers received the community newspaper as a separate newspaper thrown in their yard.

The *Chronicle* had a different advertising rate for each community newspaper but offered a combination rate when an ad was purchased in three or more community newspapers.

The ad rates for each newspaper could vary significantly and was cumbersome for ad sales reps to sell ads at the different rates. After some study of sales records, it was noted that most of the reps had sidestepped the varying newspaper rates by selling several community newspaper ads to get the bundled rate.

The *Chronicle* then streamlined the system so that an ad in any community newspaper could be purchased for the same rate. This had the benefit of making the sales effort less complicated, the billing and accounting easier to accomplish and understand and improving sales volume and profit margins.

Bundled Pricing to Increase Sales

Bundled pricing is an excellent way to increase sales volume, create a stronger relationship with customers and provide a barrier to competitors.

The most viable market for a new product offering is a firm's established customer base. The sales relationship already exists, and there is trust between the customer and the firm. A new product introduced by the firm will receive the benefit of this relationship, but there may need to be an additional incentive for customers to purchase the new product. One approach is to provide a discount for the new product and existing product or both when there is a combined purchase. Insurance companies, Internet, and telecommunications companies, to name a few, use this approach.

This approach has the added benefit of discouraging customers from switching to competing brands because the customer would lose a discount and the competitor would find it difficult to match the discount with just one product.

Houston Chronicle *and* ADVO *Bundled Pricing*

At the *Houston Chronicle*, there were several categories of customers that spent the majority of their ad budgets with ADVO, a direct mail company that delivered the retailer's mail circulars. ADVO offered very low rates for the very large advertisers by bundling their rates for the Houston market with other markets where the retailers operated.

To counter the multicity discounts offered by ADVO, we offered a discount when a retailer combined their in-newspaper advertising with our circular distribution and our commercial printing of the circulars. The printing discount proved to be key because the *Chronicle* could print for all of the retailer's markets and the printing discount could offset lost ADVO distribution discounts in other markets.

This strategy allowed the *Chronicle* to become a real marketing partner with the retailers. The relationships grew in several cases to the point that the *Chronicle* gave advice that provided a full array of marketing support programs including digital photography, graphic production consulting, and sales training.

Lessons Learned

The importance of pricing can be lost when faced with aggressive competition, financial challenges, or a changing industry landscape, but it is important to remember that pricing can be as important as any marketing strategy employed when positioning your company.

It is important to understand that pricing does not stand-alone from the other elements of marketing such as product design, distribution, and promotion, but rather, pricing helps define the value of those attributes.

Revenues and profits that could be realized by unique design, distribution, and promotion based on quality can be lost when the pricing strategy is poorly employed.

CHAPTER 10

Place

Where should my product be available to maximize sales and profits? Answering this question will have a large impact on a firm's ability to succeed. Again, if research is conducted on the targeted audience using the Consumer Adoption Drivers discussed in the chapter on Products and Services (Chapter 7), then a better understanding of the importance of place in the overall marketing strategy can be determined.

For example, Search Time Intensity, if scored low, suggests that customers are not willing to spend a lot of time to find the "right" product or the "best" price. This would indicate that convenience is very important. Products fitting in this category can be banking services or items sold at corner convenience stores. If Search Time Intensity scores high, customers are willing to spend more time searching for the right product or price and convenience is less important.

Locating the Right Place on the Internet

With the advent of the Internet, the ability to make products and services available to targeted markets has been improved. Even so businesses operating on the Internet still must make it easy for the targeted customer base to locate the enterprise and make it easy to conduct business. And some products, due to other CAD factors do not lend themselves to Internet marketing.

The first Internet requirement of making the business easy to locate requires an understanding of the job the customer is hiring the business to perform. The better this is understood, the easier it will be to identify key words that can be used in search engines. For most companies' products, the key words that can be used are numerous because the products are polymorphous perverse—have many different uses. A clothing retailer might use key search words like clothing, dress for success, evening wear, formal wear, casual clothes, and latest fashions.

The second Internet requirement of making it easy to conduct business requires basic market research. To make the Internet site "customer friendly," it is necessary to spend time understanding the customer and perhaps "walking in their shoes."

Easy Interaction Is a Component of Placement Strategy

Whether it is getting into or out of a parking lot or easily conducting business on the Internet, ease of customer interaction is critical.

Most of us have been to a website or tried to use an automated telephone program that was nothing but frustrating. I can recall a circulation automated customer service program installed at the *Houston Chronicle*. The system allowed individuals to start and stop subscription service and ask for redelivery of missed newspapers. I decided to call the system one day to see how it worked. The program was fairly straightforward and was focused on saving manpower costs, not serving customers. For example, if a customer wanted to stop delivery, the system noted the customer's name and account number and proceeded to stop delivery.

It did not allow a customer to identify problems or seek solutions. It excelled at ending business relationships.

From a marketer's point of view, a customer wishing to end a business relationship is a person to talk to. This is an opportunity to determine whether there were problems with the product or service.

In this case I changed the system to send customers wishing to stop delivery directly to a senior customer service specialist. This allowed us to determine whether there was a problem that we could act on immediately and if there was something we could do to save this customer.

Customer Traffic Origination Can Affect Marketing Strategy

For businesses wishing to use the Internet, it is important to understand why a customer would use a website to conduct business and then design the website around the customers' needs.

Understanding SFGate Web Traffic Data

The *San Francisco Chronicle*'s website is SFGate. The managers of SFGate regularly reported that their unique visitors were higher than almost all other newspapers in the United States. This concerned me a bit because the site was generating small revenues and no profit.

A little investigation revealed the reason there were so many visitors to the site because of the popularity of San Francisco as a travel destination and SFGate regularly came to the top of the search list when San Francisco was queried on the Internet search engines. Unfortunately, this traffic did not provide a means of generating robust revenues.

Further investigation allowed us to understand what was important to people in the Bay Area who regularly used the Internet. To increase revenues we had to develop programs of interest for individuals in the Bay Area. We found that entertainment, wine, food, and classified listings were of interest. With the proper focus we were able to significantly improve the traffic from individuals living in the Bay Area.

While Internet commerce continues to grow, there are, however, many instances where a business manager must pay particular attention to the physical location of business outlets.

Physical Locations

Convenience still plays a critical role in the physical location for businesses, such as restaurants, banks, and grocery stores.

HEB Location Strategy

HEB Grocery Company is a privately owned chain of grocery stores operating in Texas and Mexico. The firm is just over 100 years old and is the dominant grocer in a large portion of Texas.

HEB faced competition from a large number of local and national grocery chains in central and south Texas. A&P, Kroger, Safeway, and Albertson's were the primary national chains in these areas.

In Texas, there has been significant economic growth. Neighborhood demographics have changed and new suburbs continue to be developed.

Recognizing the market shifts, HEB closed old stores in many neighborhoods and replaced them with newer facilities and opened new stores in the growing suburban areas. The new stores offered the latest features, such as delis, in-store bakeries, and expanded general merchandise offerings. In addition, the new stores offered features that matched with the neighborhood demographics.

The major chains competing in the same markets, for the most part, did not build or relocate their stores to accommodate the changes in the marketplace. As a result, at least in part, A&P, Safeway, Kroger and Albertson's no longer have any operations in south and central Texas. Today this area is completely dominated by HEB Grocery Company.

HEB continues to review and revitalize store locations to recognize individual neighborhood demographics. This process has helped maintain market leadership.

Using Established Networks to Reach Key Markets at APD

American Property Data (APD) was a company founded with the idea that new approaches to helping investors locate prime commercial property could improve the efficacy of the commercial real estate industry.

The key to making the APD system work was to have prime commercial real estate as part of the system's inventory. This inventory would attract quality real estate investors. Matching key investors with properties that fit their investing profiles would attract more property and provide a solid revenue stream.

Because most of the prime commercial real estate was located in large metropolitan markets and represented by successful commercial real estate brokers, it was important to have key commercial brokers in key markets enter their real estate inventories into the APD system.

To attract these brokers, APD offered market exclusivity. The APD affiliate in the market would have access to APD inventory across the country as well as key investors that subscribed to the APD services.

This approach proved successful, and in about 2 years, APD grew to have representation in most major cities in the United States.

CHAPTER 11

The Successful Business

Understanding the need to meld the management functions of planning, organizing, directing, and controlling with the marketing functions of price, place, product and promotions is essential to having a successful enterprise.

HEB Grocery Company Approach

I have long admired HEB's marketing prowess. This company has consistently kept the customer's needs in focus and has changed its retail outlets to match the changing needs and demographics of the markets in which it operates.

What makes HEB so special is its management's ability to support the marketing efforts with superior management techniques. As mentioned in earlier chapters, attention given to cash and inventory management provided competitive advantages that kept costs low and provided the ability to offer low pricing to consumers.

In addition, HEB has developed human resource programs that instill loyalty and motivate their employees.

I have worked for HEB as an employee and as a consultant, and, in my opinion, the leadership of the company is focused on success through attracting the best people and giving them the best direction based on quality planning. The planning is based on constant market analysis and understanding what they must do to be successful. The ability to support leading marketing concepts with solid management techniques has provided an edge in making HEB successful.

For example, in the 1980s, HEB tried a small store format in the Houston market called HEB Pantry stores. This was developed as a way of "testing the waters" of the Houston market, which was new to HEB.

It was also a way of testing a new format that was successfully being used by Food Lion in the southeast United States.

This willingness to test new formats has allowed HEB to study their markets with innovative models. HEB's Central Market concept combines food presentation concepts from all over the world. These stores are located in major cities but provide a laboratory to develop processes and products that can be transferred to the conventional HEB stores.

While the marketing provides ideas and direction, it is superior management techniques that provide successful execution and implementation of those ideas.

American Property Data's Failure

American Property Data (APD) was based on an innovative idea. There was considerable marketing research conducted to validate the idea that a national commercial real estate market could be created through the use of computer technology.

The planning for the company was solid as was the management team. Control systems tracked all systems and resources.

The marketing approach used by APD attracted quality commercial real estate brokers and investors from across the country.

There was a key point that marketing research failed to uncover and that was the exclusive listings held by commercial real estate brokers. Exclusive listings meant that the broker representing this property would receive the exclusive right to market the property and collect the commission. This was different from properties that were made available to the open market and would require brokers to share the commission.

Commercial brokers did not want to put their exclusive listings in the APD system but did put nonexclusive properties in the system. Thus APD did not have access to some of the most desirable properties being offered. This problem was not insurmountable but became difficult when coupled with the lack of available financing for the ongoing operations. In the end, APD's founders could not continue funding the company and sold it to a key commercial broker in Boston.

In this case, APD did not enjoy the success it could have because a few of the principles mentioned in this book were not employed. One of the chief reasons the firm did not do well was not having sufficient money available for the start-up phase.

Newspapers' Challenges

The newspaper industry, for years, was extremely profitable and well managed. This industry has been affected by a market disruption and is struggling to find a means to protect its business model and compete against the new world of Internet journalism and advertising. The industry is changing and technology is having a profound effect. As the following discussion illustrates, solutions for this industry may need to be radical but by using proven principles, these solutions can be evaluated and implemented successfully.

A New Approach for the San Francisco Chronicle

San Francisco is one of the most competitive media markets in the United States. When I was named EVP and general manager of the *San Francisco Chronicle*, Hearst had just purchased the *Chronicle* and sold their newspaper (the *San Francisco Examiner*).

My job was to try to rebuild the ad revenues and put the organization on a solid market footing.

The City of San Francisco is located at the end of a peninsula and is restricted topographically from expanding. Thus the population is limited and population growth was concentrated in outlying communities. Some of the communities grew rapidly and over the years had developed quality media outlets. For newspapers, the competition included the *San Jose Mercury News, Oakland Tribune*, and *Contra Costa Times*. All were quality newspapers, respected and read by the residents of their communities.

Of course over the years, other media outlets had gained strength and provided good coverage of news and the ability to distribute advertising messages.

As the population grew in surrounding communities so did the retail outlets, many were branches of retailers that started in San Francisco. Others were new retailers serving only the outlying communities.

The retailers in these outlying communities found it necessary to move part and sometimes the majority of their ad budgets to media serving the outlying communities.

Clearly the task at hand was not an easy one. Our strategy at the *Chronicle* was to introduce new products and improve coverage of outlying communities. The *San Francisco Chronicle* had a strong franchise and a positive reputation and our efforts were rewarded to a great degree. It was however important to understand that retailers were not likely to abandon the media that helped them grow their business and served the communities they served. By the same token we could not expect that the residents of those communities would reduce the use of local media in favor of the *Chronicle*.

We began considering other options that included partnerships with other media. As we studied the options we decided, for the most part, partnerships that actually moved business our way would be short-lived because they would cause some deterioration of the partners' market share.

I visited with the folks at competing Internet sites, the area newspapers, cable operators, television, and radio stations to develop partnerships. We were able to put together a few programs that produced a modicum of success but did not change market share.

The programs that changed market share recognized the competition and targeted the audience that we intended to serve. These included a marriage mail concept I had introduced while in Houston, a new wine section (we after all were in wine country), revamping the entertainment section for the *Sunday Chronicle* and introducing new Internet revenue programs.

As I mentioned earlier, partnerships are not likely to produce market shifting results and over time would become one sided and therefore come to an end. Today unilateral action recognizing the value placed on the competition is in order.

I might, for example, offer consumers low rates for putting Internet classifieds placed in competing media in my newspaper and on my website. This has the danger of moving some of my customers to the competition unless the pricing and marketing were clearly thought-out. It would almost certainly provide better results for consumers and businesses.

This idea sounds radical when compared with conventional marketing strategy approaches. In this example, Internet classified ad sites would get additional traffic from ads in my newspaper and on my website that identified merchandise listed on their websites. Those websites might also be able to raise their rates due to increased demand.

The positive side is that I would have the ads on my website and directional ads and revenue in my newspaper that I do not have today and would not likely get. I would also have a new beachhead from which to drive new marketing initiatives.

For retail advertisers spending a large amount of the ad budget in the competing newspapers, I might let them count the dollars spent with the competition toward ad volume contract pricing I offered.

In this case the retailers getting volume contract discounts for advertising placed with competing media would expand their reach at discounted ad rates. This has the danger of having my current customers move more dollars to competing media and actually get a lower rate with my newspaper. So the rate discounts would have to require growth in ad spending in my newspaper.

While these approaches are uncommon they do recognize the new market realities and offer an approach to shift market share if well thought out.

To insure that these ideas are appropriate I would go through the product planning processes outlined in Part II, Chapter 7 of this book and use research based on the CAD. I would use cross-functional teams and the standards of performance programs outlined in Part I, Chapter 2 to implement the ideas that are developed into programs. The programs implemented would be monitored for quality control. Reporting and feedback systems would be needed to provide managers with information on the impact of the programs and to provide corrective actions if needed.

In today's hypercompetitive and hypershifting landscape the solutions that will move market share and win stable relationships with consumer and business communities will be based on the realities of why the competition exists and the long and short-term roles they play in the marketplace. Approaches to improve a company's standing in the market must be customer focused and develop strategies based on programs to align business goals with market needs.

The Successful Business

The business that is successful today and will be successful tomorrow will use all of the principles outlined in this book to plan and execute on-going operations and to introduce new products and services. It is a disciplined use of these principles combined with the best information available on the market that will allow managers to navigate through difficult markets and to prosper when the market is robust.

Notes

Chapter 2

1. American Management Association (1973).
2. Christensen (1997), pp. 207–211.

Chapter 3

1. Randazzo (1976).
2. Randazzo (1976).

Chapter 7

1. Christensen and Raynor (2003), pp. 75–78. Christensen suggests that product development focus should be on the job a customer hires a firm to do rather than on the customer.
2. Zaltman (1973), pp. 93–115. The CAD was developed based on Gerald Zaltman's research on social phenomenon.
3. This flow chart and the process was developed by Gary Randazzo.

Chapter 8

1. Newspaper Association of America—2012.

References

American Management Association. (1973). *How to improve managerial performance*, New York, NY: AMACOM.

Christensen, C. (1997). *The innovator's dilemma.* Cambridge, MA: Harvard Business Press.

Christensen, C., & Raynor, M. (2003). *The innovator's solution.* Cambridge, MA: HBS Press, pp. 75–85.

Newspaper Association of America—2012, www.naa.org/trends and numbers/ readership, August 29, 2012

Maslow, A. (1943). A theory of human motivation. *Psychological Review.* 50.

Randazzo, G. (1976). *Effectiveness of an interest penalty to control cash in a multi-retail outlet corporation.* Corpus Christi, TX: Texas A&M University.

Zaltman, G. (1973). *Processes and phenomena of social change.* Hoboken, NJ: Wiley Interscience, pp. 93–115.

Index

OTHER TITLES IN THE ENTREPRENEURSHIP AND SMALL BUSINESS MANAGEMENT COLLECTION

Scott Shane, Case Western University, Collection Editor

Announcing the Business Expert Press Digital Library

Concise E-books Business Students Need for Classroom and Research

This book can also be purchased in an e-book collection by your library as
- a one-time purchase,
- that is owned forever,
- allows for simultaneous readers,
- has no restrictions on printing, and
- can be downloaded as PDFs from within the library community.

Our digital library collections are a great solution to beat the rising cost of textbooks. e-books can be loaded into their course management systems or onto student's e-book readers.

The **Business Expert Press** digital libraries are very affordable, with no obligation to buy in future years. For more information, please visit **www.businessexpertpress.com/librarians**. To set up a trial in the United States, please contact **Adam Chesler** at *adam.chesler@businessexpertpress.com* for all other regions, contact **Nicole Lee** at *nicole.lee@igroupnet.com*.